SAIL ON, O SHIP OF STATE

—

*Edited by Johanna Möhring
and Gwythian Prins*

Thou, too, sail on, O Ship of State!
Sail on, O Union, strong and great!
Humanity with all its fears,
With all the hopes of future years,
Is hanging breathless on thy fate!

– Henry Wadsworth Longfellow

Notting Hill Editions

Published in 2013
by Notting Hill Editions Ltd
Newcombe House, 45 Notting Hill Gate
London W11 3LQ

Designed by FLOK Design, Berlin, Germany
Typeset by CB editions, London

Printed and bound
by Memminger MedienCentrum, Memmingen, Germany

A CIP record for this book
is available from the British Library

ISBN 978-1-907-90359-5

www.nottinghilleditions.com

Contents

Rt. Hon. Michael Gove, MP,
Secretary of State for Education

– Preface –

'You are pitiful, isolated individuals! You are bankrupts! Your role is played out! Go where you belong from now on – into the dustbin of history!'

When Leon Trotsky first invoked the dustbin of history to anathematise the Mensheviks in 1917 in these arrogantly self-confident words, he can hardly have imagined that it would be his ideas – and on a larger scale yet, those of Karl Marx which had inspired him – that would be among those to be most firmly consigned to time's trashcan. Marxism, like feudalism, nazism, paganism, anti-nomianism, Jansenism, apartheid, Juche and Gaddafi's Third Way, is now an ideology so discredited and deadbeat that not even the most avid recycler can fashion something useful from its wreckage.

It is striking that so many of those ideologies which have claimed to be validated by scientific or historical inevitability have been rendered so comprehensively false and obsolete by the advance of knowledge and the progress of time. What is just as striking, though less observed, is that those political ideas which have made humbler claims for themselves, and thus were often considered pallid things with poor prospects, have endured.

A belief in Liberal Education, Parliamentary Democracy and Fiscal Conservatism, at various times in the last century, would have marked any individual out as hopelessly romantic in the face of economic realities, pathetically wedded to compromise when man needed bold decisions and swift actions to make progress, and dully imaginative in the face of new financial paradigms. But these political ideas have endured because they are – in their flexibility, their room for adjustment to circumstance, their rootedness in our experience – reflective of human nature.

Mankind is naturally thirsty for knowledge, naturally disposed to see wisdom emerge from debate, and everywhere inclined to see the folly in imagining that greed and fear can be banished from human hearts.

There is, however, one political idea which has been even more abused over time than these three, even more firmly consigned to posterity's binbag, even more ridiculed and pronounced redundant.

The nation state

It has become a commonplace of political argument that nation states are historical anomalies – appropriate for their time in the nineteenth century as successor regimes to absolute monarchies, sprawling empires and petty principalities – but hopelessly ill-equipped for contemporary challenges.

When so many of today's problems – from climate change to pandemics, migratory flows to capital flight – cross borders how can a single nation state provide its citizens with protection?

If nation states exist to share risk amongst a population – by providing them with a common defence and common social security system in which all have an interest – surely bigger would be better . . . ?

Does not the additional muscle that comes from membership of a trans-national EU provide our people with better protection? And are not global institutions like the World Bank required to save nations from their own folly?

Those inclined to defend the nation state are reminded, gently and not so gently, that their preferred model of governance had its roots in the ethnic determinism of a darker age – do we really want to return to a time when Germany was for the Germans, when Spain was one and holy, when a French officer could be thought a likely traitor just because he was not a Christian? Nation states are, we are told, by their very nature exclusive. Borders keep things – people, ideas, modernity – out.

But to associate the nation state with the terrible crimes of the last hundred years is to miss all the lessons history can teach us. It was totalitarianism, which bewitched men's minds and unleashed such terrible slaughter. Whether it was Stalinism or Hitlerism, the demented Marxist nihilism of Pol Pot or the jihadist

Islamism of today, the ideologies which inspired such hate were nothing to do with the principles which guided men like Macaulay or Mazzini, Alexander Hamilton or Alexis de Tocqueville.

Nation states emerged as political systems which could reconcile the fellow feeling necessary for shared sacrifice with the openness to change necessary for growth. The welfare state – universal healthcare and education, the transfer of wealth from rich to poor, working adults to young and old alike – is a child of the nation state. It depends upon a feeling of solidarity, which is only sustainable within an identifiable community defined by shared values.

And it is the sharing of values – and of language and culture – within one political system which makes not just the transfer of wealth but the exercise of legitimate authority possible. The discussions we need to have to ensure power is exercised fairly, the checks we need to erect to stop power being used arbitrarily, the conventions which make judges fair and elections free, are all only possible when there is a community of shared assumptions, traditions and language. For democracy to work properly it has to be within a nation state.

And there is nothing either introspective or insular about nation states. Quite the opposite. Only democratic nation states have the resilience to be able to cope with migratory movements without descending into communalism and strife. Only democratic nation states have the confidence, and trust, in their armed forces which allows them to play a noble role on a wider stage. Only democratic nation states have the economic traditions which allow them to be truly free-trading and therefore the drivers of global growth.

It is the existence of nation states which ensures political dissidents can claim asylum, the Jewish people can be safe at last, mankind can continually experiment with new ways of generating prosperity and freedom will always find a home. That is why it is such a pleasure to welcome the essays in this timely book, whose authors seek to renovate the study of the nation state. And I cannot emphasise sufficiently just how timely their work is. Around the world – even in Europe, where the European project of ever-closer union was supposed to have extinguished the constituent states of the old continent – under pressure of crisis we observe how allegiance to their nation states is pre-eminent in the hearts of most peoples. This book brings together a range of distinguished voices to explore just why the nation state should be such a durable – and valuable – construct.

I am delighted that the London School of Economics provided a congenial home for the research project of which this book is the product. In particular I am grateful to Professor Gwythian Prins, Research Professor of the School, and Ms Johanna Möhring, Visiting Fellow, who drove this project. They were willing to embrace an agenda which, when this work began, was quite eccentric to the conventional wisdoms of the University world, although less so by the day, I am pleased to observe. Assisted by their colleagues in Oxford and St Andrews, Professors Biggar and Rengger, they have recruited the star-studded team whose thoughts are to be found in these pages.

I am also enormously grateful to the generous sponsor of this project, Mr Tom Kremer – a polymathic Transylvanian refugee who was welcomed by Britain after the War and who, like George Soros, is both a philanthropist and himself a thinker and writer on these matters, as his earlier book, *The Missing Heart of Europe*, and his chapter here demonstrate.

We need to redress the skewed agendas of the last decades. We need to reclaim the nation state as a public good. These are tasks engaged in this book.

Johanna Möhring and Gwythian Prins

– Sail On, O Ship of State –

'People only accept change when they are faced with necessity
and only recognise necessity when a crisis is upon them.'
– Jean Monnet

'If you want to be right in the future, you have to
occasionally accept not to be in fashion.'
– Ernest Renan, 'What is a Nation?'
Lecture at Sorbonne, 11 March 1882

D ecisive moments of transition and transformation in history have an annoying habit of revealing their identities clearly only after the event. When a
war has broken out, or a Berlin Wall has fallen, their
very decisiveness can seem to be boringly consensual
to general opinion – after the event. But if we want
to chart the tides of events reliably, we have to stare
history in the face, recognise and describe what is happening as – or before – it happens.

For more than two intellectual generations, since
1945, there has been an ascendant narrative in international affairs which has represented the nation state as
pathological in its very nature. It has blamed the nation
states of Europe for the double catastrophes of the

First and Second World Wars and has invested hope in a new post-nation state world order which arose from those ashes. That order was expressed in novel over-arching political structures and in idealistic and previously untried ideologies of political association. Serious study of the nation state has been scorned in political discourse and has withered in the universities. Meanwhile Western academic acclaim for the ascendancy of a new world, deemed cosmopolitan and supranational, as well as post-ideological and post-religious, has flourished.

But in 2013 we are plainly in the midst of a crisis for that sixty-years-old narrative. For a decade at least, all the main multilateral institutions have been simultaneously but differently waning. The UN, founded as a collective security organisation after the Second World War, has faded steadily as it proved incapable in crisis after crisis of defending its Charter principles under duress. The failure to agree Kofi Annan's reforms of the Security Council in 2004 was a defining moment. NATO's fading relevance as military alliance linking North America and Europe has been cruelly brought to light in the wars in Afghanistan. The EU project of ever-closer union is fracturing under the strains of a systemic economic and financial crisis. Economic globalisation, with all its benefits, stands revealed as more puzzling and less of a panacea than the cosmopolitan globalisation narrative credited. And contrary to expectations of a largely secular and post-modern European elite, both ethnic nationalism and religion remain major ideological driving forces – and not just in global politics. To the surprise of many, those forces have re-surfaced in our midst.

This is not to deny that the 'Ship of State' is not facing strong headwinds. But against the predictions (and hopes) of many, the affection that citizens feel for their national identities, and loyalty to state forms, which they believe represent them, has not waned. Rather, it has waxed as global troubles have loomed. It commands the loyalty of citizens who conversely withhold legitimacy from some of the newer creations, which claim their allegiance. The nation state has refused to shuffle off the stage of history. As Longfellow would not be surprised to find, fears and hopes of humanity continue to be tied to its fate. Why? With what implications? These are core questions that are explored in this book.

Certainly, history offers ample sad proof that when totalitarian ideologies manage to tap the state's concentrated means of violence, murderous energy can be unleashed within and without. Yet in the darkest periods of the last century, the same state structures that were captured by fascists and communists also acted as citizens' guardians in free societies. National allegiance rallied the strength necessary to endure immense hardships. Even in Stalin's Russia it was no accident that the titanic military effort of the Soviet Union on the eastern front, which smashed the heart out of the Nazi military machine, was summonsed by an appeal to defend Mother Russia, not to defend an ideology. Then and ever since in Russia, it has been called the Great Patriotic War.

In the decades following the Second World War, awareness of the positive powers of national states was almost completely eclipsed by the dominant narrative of blame for the catastrophe that had just been endured. This was true not only in Germany, which understandably sought to atone for its role and to bind itself within a supra-national entity, but was true also quite widely among the occupied continental European states. While never entering the general public mind, the narrative of blame attached to the nation state also attracted a segment of the British governing class including Edward Heath, the prime minister who took Great Britain into what was then the 'Common Market'. Attempts were made to dilute citizens' affection for their nation states' societal bonds. Sovereign powers were continually transferred from national jurisdictions to international and supra-national institutions.

This book has come about because there is a strong case to be made that we are again at a decisive turning point in international affairs. In February 2012, the Mackinder Programme at the London School of Economics, the McDonald Centre for Theology, Ethics and Public Life at the University of Oxford and the Department of International Affairs at the University of St Andrews organised an international conference to discuss the state of the nation state. It brought together academics, analysts, policymakers and journalists from Europe and North America. This collection of essays arising from that event is a first attempt to reconstruct and renovate a debate about the future of the nation state in the conditions of the present and plausible future world. It is constructed to take equally seriously more than one route into the future and more than one account of how we come to be where we are today.

Why has this not been a time of the breaking of nations, but rather of the breaking of those eager successors, keen to push the old structures aside? In the first part of this book, 'The nation state and us', the reader is invited to ponder the reasons for the persistence of the nation state. It explores the values it embodies and the purposes it serves, as well as the sources of affection that it engenders. In this section, different forms of nation state are addressed for there is no single meaning for the term. In the second part of the book, 'Breaking up or sticking together', the inevitable issues of secession and of staying together are discussed.

'Losing and finding our history', the third part, starts from an awareness that history can be a battlefield: that control of the historical narrative is a potent weapon and that whoever controls it can suppress or enhance different views. This weapon has been consciously wielded by those who would slay the nation state in form and in the minds of people. Control of the historical narrative in schools has been a prime battleground. Therefore it is important to discuss the role of history and national historical narrative. What are the different ways in which national histories are and should be presented? Why has popular affection for the nation state persisted rather than died?

Parts four and five, 'Cosmopolitanism and its discontents' and 'Decline (and fall?) of international governance', address the intellectual and instrumental aspects of the cosmopolitan globalisation agenda, respectively. They consider the sources of the desire for supra- and international regimes and the reasons for its current problems.

The nation state and us

For most of recorded history, empires, city states, religious orders or feudal masters – distinctively non-national forms of governance – have been the order of the day. That nation states, let alone democratic ones, should one day be perceived as the norm rather than the exception is quite an astonishing development. A millennium ago, nobody would have expected their emergence; and to predict, in a world of fiefdoms, kingdoms and empires, that this form of collective life would one day be ubiquitous, would have seemed astonishing. Empires could have persisted; the feudal system could have stayed the prevailing mode of social organisation; city states could have upheld their dominance lacing

6

Europe with their economic ties; and celestial, rather than worldly powers could have prevailed in the fight over whose authority reigned supreme on this earth. Yet over almost a thousand years, nation states came into existence in Europe and evolved into many different variations of the same theme. From the European crucible, since 1500 they have spread to almost every part of the globe, first via colonial expansion as annexes to their mother country. With decolonisation in the middle of last century, those entities became nominally independent national states themselves. Only look at the proliferating flags of the nations parading at the Olympic Games and the enthusiasms which national pride engender and it is evident how well rooted those implants have become. Indeed, the nation state is not an artificial Western political and cultural concept imposed on a hapless periphery. Quite the contrary. A unique combination of factors, together with many a historic twist may have allowed the nation state to appear on the scene only in Western Europe. But as an export product, it has had unrivalled success. It has been welcomed with open arms because its features, combining political legitimacy with a sovereign territorial unit, strongly resonate with popular aspirations around the world.

To answer the question why the nation state has persisted and what functions it has performed in the recent past, **Michael Ignatieff** considers four moments since 1945. Colonial liberation after the Second World

War brought the guarantee of sovereignty and independent statehood. For the first time in history, millions of people around the world were given a way to actively shape their future. A second significant moment of the nation state occurred in the 1970s, when democratic revolutions driven by peoples mobilising against authoritarian regimes spread democracy to southern Europe. The break-up of the Soviet Union in 1991 made possible the emancipation and rise of captive nations and unleashed tremendous enthusiasm for democracy expressed in nations variously constructed or even re-animated after seeming euthanasia in the Soviet era. Ignatieff ends on a sombre note with the economic and financial crisis of 2008, which heralds the era of sovereign default. Since the end of the second world war, markets have outgrown national sovereigns, yet populations turn to the nation state for answers in times of crisis. It remains to be seen whether the state is able to wrestle power back from the markets.

In these stressful and dark times, there is one frame of reference invested with trust and affection to which individuals seem reflexively to turn. Far from being broken or universally malign, nation states command the affection and loyalty of free peoples. They alone can confer whole-hearted legitimacy to public action. Nation states are the frame of almost every aspect of our very existence, be it political, social or cultural; they form the building blocks of international relations. Yet we often forget quite how singular they are. Recognising and regularising the difference between private and public life, between church and state, between man and citizen, has been the fundamental achievement of the European state. This distinction allowed for the foundation of a polity ruled by the laws of men for men. Yet without the predominant influence of Judeo-Christian culture, man – created in God's image – and the sanctity of individual human life would have never become the cornerstone of political action. It was the struggle between sword and cross, as well as those deeply held religious beliefs, that allowed for the creation of both rights and duties tying together European states and their citizens in a remarkable fashion.

Roger Scruton argues that the national idea is the very basis for our modern democratic state, as it pushes back pre-political loyalties to make room for the Enlightenment on a defined territory. In Europe, unconditional loyalties, which tend to be a matter of identity and attachment rather than agreement, almost always take a national form. For most, national sentiment is the only shared motive that will justify sacrifice in the common cause. The capacity for self-sacrifice is a precondition of enduring communities. He argues that it is proximity, not reason, that creates charitable feeling between people and that association within the boundaries of the nation state provides the best defence against take-over by rampant ideologies of one sort or another.

Breaking up or sticking together

The conceptual beginnings of the modern nation state are often located in the publication of Thomas Hobbes's *Leviathan* in 1651. *Leviathan* describes the basic building blocks of the state as we conceive of it today. It prefigures definition of the state as holder of the legitimate monopoly of violence (the 'nightwatchman' functions of the state) as later described by the German sociologist Max Weber. Hobbes described a centralised structure able to impose unchallenged control over a given territory, thereby ending a state of permanent warfare of each man against the other and thereby making possible the origins of civil society.

Jean Bethke Elshtain stresses the importance of territorial inviolability and internal coherence. Civic identity is meaningful only within a delineated political space within which citizens can deliberate and act together. Divisions across ethnic, cultural or religious lines erode the very principle of having to find common ground across differences inside a polis. Splitting up into ever-smaller entities contributes to systemic instability, as it whets the appetites of bigger states to impose their will on defenceless entities.

But what if a constituent part of a nation state would like to go its own way? Should those exclusive bonds holding states together in empires ever be questioned? **Daniel Hannan** firmly believes so. National loyalties form the very basis for democracy, so movements by nations to secede deserve a better press. International institutions oppose the national principles holding up instead the multinational federal state as an end in itself and as a means to suppress nation states. They are prepared to invest considerable resources in ensuring that state borders don't coincide with ethnographic ones. Why? Because international bodies, such as the EU rest on the idea that national loyalties are arbitrary, transient and discreditable.

Losing and finding our history

Whether national feelings of loyalty are arbitrary or not is certainly of more than academic interest. With the jury still out, history should be a good place to start exploring the matter. A nation state occupies not only a defined territory but also a distinct place in history and, as earlier noted, in the minds and the hearts of citizens. History has the almost magic capacity to transform individuals from being mere subjects to active participants in the affairs of their country.

Chris Husbands writes on the crucial role that history and historians play in this respect. When it comes to the nation state, history cannot simply be disaggregated and harvested for bits and pieces meant to usefully inform the prejudices – any prejudices – of the present. History is scattered with dangerous examples of such hijackings. Equally, the balance between the focus on evaluation of evidence and the seizing of a sense of narrative is disturbed at our peril. History challenges us to look beyond what is happening to what might be going on.

In theory well placed to enlighten our thinking, in practice history currently cannot be accessed to inform our debate on the nation state. By conscious design, we have amputated ourselves from our past. Certainly, no country can claim innocence; seen from our vantage point of the beginning of the twenty-first century, our pasts are more or less littered with crimes of various sorts. With populations around the world emerging literally shell-shocked from the Second World War, opponents of the nation state were able to condemn all past as tainted. By that account, events starting in 1914 and ending in 1945 form a watershed – everything that happened before is interpreted as leading directly and inexorably to the trenches and the ramps of the extermination camps. Beyond, for them, paradise beckons; salvation can be reached by leaving our past firmly behind. But far from liberating us, this sanitised, uniform post-national narrative leaves us in a limbo, stuck in time with no legitimate way of change. What cannot be denied is that differences, often irreconcilable ones, exist and persist between states and cultures. They ought to be cherished, not to be denied, as they form the very basis for human liberty and diversity.

And it is with these thoughts that we turn to the eccentric island that is, in Churchill's famous phrase, 'with but not of Europe'. In his essay, **Frank Field** explores what it is about the achievement and vitality of the English constitution that has kept England exceptional. With the help of the peerless writings of Walter Bagehot, he reviews how the wider identity of the United Kingdom came to be, and the latent problems that have recently surfaced; for Field warns that the system is under threat from devolution, which is neglecting the legitimate concerns of the English people. In Field's analysis, applying Bagehot's insights to the modern moment, there may be trouble ahead for England and the other parties in the currently United Kingdom.

Cosmopolitanism and its discontents

Dreams of a peaceful coexistence transcending the state system are almost as old as states themselves. Cosmopolitanism, the idea of supranational governance for the benefit of all humanity, strongly resonates with our most deeply held beliefs about the commonality and community of mankind. It encourages us to believe that we are meant to live as one, united in brotherly love, but that we are held artificially apart by national boundaries. Throughout the centuries, it has inspired political action in various ideological guises, variously religiously or ideologically motivated. It has been the idealised endpoint of a teleological interpretation of world history, as seen through both Christian and Marxist spectacles.

How states should interact, what rules should apply in war and in peacetime, has preoccupied mankind ever since the emergence of state entities. In the absence of a supreme power installing and guarding perpetual peace, attempts were made to bind states by collective rules instead, at least to mediate the most destructive aspects of interstate conflict. Gathering speed with the spread of literacy and means of communication, a body of law emerged codifying such rules, with canny statecraft sitting uneasily side by side with moral principles rooted in religion. Technological progress and the industrialisation of warfare in the nineteenth century reinforced tendencies to limit state sovereignty. Animated by the ever more deadly struggle between the great powers in the twentieth century, cosmopolitanism gained in supporters. Even though it has spectacularly failed in establishing world peace, it has managed to hold the moral high ground and to set the terms of debate in international relations for the last sixty years.

Michael Lind critically explores the current state of play for this resonant concept. Over the last twenty years, many on both sides of the Atlantic came to believe that the nation state was fading in importance. National political identities and allegiances were expected to be gradually replaced by global ones. Economic globalisation was supposed to be matched by global political integration. Now, the cosmopolitan bubble, it would seem, has burst. The world is likely to remain divided among great sovereign powers for ages to come. But cosmopolitanism has not simply been a quaint, harmless religious faith held by global elites. It has resulted in multiple failures, from the Kyoto Protocol on climate policy to flawed development aid programmes, among others.

But is cosmopolitanism really condemned to end up on the dust heap of history? States do not exist in a void, after all. State sovereignty holds in itself the realisation of interdependence, even for the *primus inter pares*. **Garrett Wallace-Brown** believes that cosmopolitanism has become the victim of an unwelcome divorce. In his essay he argues that a suspended conversation between cosmopolitanism and the nation state should be reopened. For almost two academic generations, cosmopolitanism has been wedded to various speculative projects for utopian supra-national governance. Implied within this has been some generalised moral hostility to the state. The challenge today is to reacquaint sovereignty with cosmopolitanism by introducing the concept of cosmopolitan responsible states: States who increase their self-determination via international engagement. Patriotism, he argues, could be based on cosmopolitan values and universal duties. These should not be enemies but allies.

Decline (and fall?) of international governance

The signing of the Peace of Westphalia is usually taken to mark the beginning of the modern state system. In 1648, treaties officially ended the Thirty Years' War that had devastated larges swathes of the Holy Roman Empire. They also concluded the Eighty Years' War between Spain and the Dutch Republic, which officially gained its independence. Even though Spain and France continued hostilities for another decade, the treaties marked a turning point. A system arose based on two dimensions of sovereignty: one recognising state authority within a distinct territory and population and the other, the right to the inviolability of boundaries. The concept was revolutionary because it anchored states as legitimate actors in international relations, while at the same time laying the first foundations for representative government on a distinct national territory. It was this 'Westphalian' system that came to be blamed for the horrors of modern war.

But in addition to setting the terms for framing intellectual discussion, international and supranational ideas have been extraordinarily successful in finding institutional incarnations. The League of Nations arose from the hopes of Woodrow Wilson and the victors of the First World War, yet collapsed as soon as events put it under real strain in the Abyssinian crisis of 1936, when Mussolini's Italy invaded Ethiopia. In an attempt to learn the lessons from that failure, the United Nations was invested with a Security Council of the Great Powers intended to ensure that when the UN acted, it could avoid the fate of the League. Last, but certainly not least, faith in supranational governance profoundly animated the founders of the European project. Have either of these entities lived up to their promise?

Julian Lindley-French thinks not. Liberal internationalism is in crisis; the United Nations and the European Union are stalling as political projects, because they are incapable of dealing with contemporary challenges. They can respond to neither power in the state system nor in the market as they suffer a sovereignty deficit. Perhaps ironically, they have to rely on national states to faithfully execute their writ – which is rather like asking turkeys to vote for Christmas! The UN and the EU also suffer from a leadership deficit, as membership in those organisations has been designed to prevent any one country from dominating. And if that wasn't bad enough, in both institutions, strategic vision and diplomacy, the pillars of statecraft, are sorely missing.

What is striking upon closer inspection are not only the inherent construction flaws of the institutions outlined above. Holding up those edifices, however ramshackle, are foundations formed from vast amounts of sunk political capital. Even when confronted with abysmal failure, the statesmen involved simply cannot retreat. The costs to them of changing course are seen as forbiddingly high, trumping all benefits of looking for alternative courses of action.

Tom Kremer offers a bracing analysis of that European project which has embodied most fully the ambition of the European federal vision: the attempt to create a European currency. The 'Euro' shackles together European states which have widely differing economies and national temperaments. Jean Monnet and his close associates learned the lesson in the 1920s that lacking a popular mandate for their ambition to supplant the states of Europe, they had to use an indirect approach. Crises would force unwilling citizens to accept emergency steps towards 'ever more Europe', otherwise unacceptable in calm times. But as Kremer notes, the successes of the last sixty years have been Pyrrhic victories. The story of the euro is in essence the story of the failure of that tactic expressed in the headpiece quotation from Monnet that opens this introduction.

A safety notice

Ernest Renan, French historian, philosopher and writer, correctly observed long ago that those who disagree with the prevailing consensus ran the risk of being badly out of fashion. They could expect to be labeled war-mongers or radical pessimists or – most irritating of all – disturbers of the consensus. The contributors to this collection are not of one point of view; but all came together to debate their views, all running Renan's risk together. Traversing this difficult terrain calls for an uncommon degree of self-restraint combined with imagination; for vital issues, such as the future of the nation state, are inevitably fraught with emotion. The terrain is populated with advocates engaged in a war against other viewpoints not their own, rather than in genuine debate. The authors seek a sounder route via frank debate, from which we believe genuine fresh insight can be gained. The reader will find that while there is no regimented consensus of conclusions in the pages, which follow, there is unanimity about the importance of understanding well this moment of transition and transformation.

Part I
The Nation State and Us

Michael Ignatieff

– 1: The Nation State and the Promise of Sovereignty –

G lobalisation is sweeping away barriers of language, geography and distance that used to keep peoples apart. An expanding network of international organisations including the United Nations, the European Union, the World Trade Organisation and the International Monetary Fund, exert ever greater control over states. Many of our most serious problems – climate change and global economic instability, to name but two – are transnational in scope and impact. Be that as it may, nation states remain the locus of political loyalty and legitimacy for the world's peoples. Any authority that international organisations may have acquired, they exercise as a delegated power from nation states.

Looking at the recent history of the nation state, it's not hard to see why it is the sole political unit that continues to command ultimate political loyalty. In the period since 1945, the nation state has performed four essential functions, and its success in these roles goes a long way to explaining why it maintains its monopoly on political allegiance.

Masters in their own house

First of all, the nation state delivers self-determination. The campaigns for independence that swept through the European colonies in Africa and Asia between 1945 and the early 1970s all sought to deliver their peoples a nation state of their own. National self-determination empowered subject peoples even when it didn't lead to democracy. But even on those occasions when independence was followed by home-grown despotism, African and Asian people felt they had taken a decisive step towards becoming masters in their own house. Acquiring a nation state of their own and throwing off foreign rule were vital affirmations of their dignity and equality as peoples. If we wish to understand how racial hierarchy and racist discrimination were discredited after 1945, we should give pride of place to these movements for national independence. When under the UN charter of 1945 states were recognised as equal in dignity and rights, their peoples took the recognition of their state's sovereignty as an affirmation of their dignity as a nation. Because their new states provided a vital affirmation of their dignity, citizens of newly independent states were prepared to stick with the regimes that ruled them even when they treated them badly and disappointed their hopes.

Of the people, by the people, for the people

Independence did not always lead to democracy, but when it did, democracy strengthened the appeal of the nation state. Here is its second historical function: to link independence with democracy. The nation state gave citizens two distinct experiences of sovereignty: ejecting foreign rulers and allowing the people to chose their own leaders. This remains the core of the nation state's appeal. It promises people they will be masters in their own house.

To become masters and sovereigns, the people often have had to rise up against their own domestic oppressors. Many nation states have been born in revolution, from old democracies like France and the United States to younger ones like South Africa. New or old, the nation state legitimises itself to its people as the guardian of their revolution.

Sometimes, those who led revolutions against colonial rulers used state power to deny their people democracy and freedom. In many post-colonial states in Africa, the original liberation heroes imposed despotic rule by passing themselves off as the father of the nation. Be it Kwame Nkrumah in Ghana, Jomo Kenyatta in Kenya or Robert Mugabe in Zimbabwe, each claimed in his turn that he, not the people, incarnated the nation's struggle for independence. Each dictator's opponents in the streets asserted that the people themselves, not their autocrats, truly represented the nation.

In these political struggles to democratise ex-colonial states, the struggle was not just over who ultimately controlled state power. The battle was over who represented the identity of the nation. When democratic forces won, the nation re-asserted its control over the state. Ghanaian society, for example, freed itself from the founding father, Nkrumah and re-asserted the nation as the source of the state's legitimacy.

The capacity of autocrats to hold on to state power around the world depends on something more than pure oppression. It also turns on the degree to which they succeed in representing themselves as authentic guardians of the nation. In Cuba, for example, Castro's regime clings to power by passing itself off as the vanguard of the revolution that freed the nation. Conversely, democratic revolutions rely for their success on the degree to which the people empower themselves as protectors of the nation against the tyrannical state.

This is to say that there is national patriotism and state patriotism and that the former can be deployed to dislodge the latter. One reason why the nation state is so enduring a political form is that it carries within it the dynamic of its own renewal. Sometimes holders of state power derive legitimacy by representing themselves as the guardian of the nation. When they turn tyrannical, the nation can rise and re-assert itself as the ultimate source of legitimacy for the state.

In the democratic revolutions that swept away the last remaining dictatorships of Europe in the 1970s – in

Portugal, Spain and Greece – popular forces sought to wrest control of the state in order to return the nation to its democratic traditions. Patriots in Spain sought to return their country to the republican inheritance of the late 1920s and early 1930s and the Greeks reached back to their ancient democratic traditions and more recent battle for independence from the Turks. The Portuguese likewise sought to awaken from the Salazar dictatorship by anchoring the nation in a democratic tradition seen as European-wide. In each of these cases, the people saw themselves as the nation and answered the democratic clarion call to return the state to collective self-rule. The democratic re-assertion of control by the nation over the state was an empowering and ennobling experience for citizens and deepened their attachment to the state.

In these three European cases, each nation was relatively homogeneous, with common religious and demographic conditions, and therefore had the capacity to mobilise as a united force against tyranny. In most other nation states, however, different nations share the same state but do not necessarily share the same interests in relation to it. There are slightly fewer than 200 states in the world today and up to 5,000 groups claiming the status of nation, whether by virtue of ethnicity, language, historical fate or geographic concentration.

In multinational states, the function of the central state is to hold different peoples together in a common civic pact. The state's legitimacy is dependent on being not the guardian of a single nation, but the guarantor of the equality of all the nations who compose it.

Living together

The third historical function of the nation state, therefore, has been to enable different nations to live together under the same political roof. Where this breaks down, the mono-national nation state re-emerges to protect ethnic minorities who break away and seek the security of a state of their own.

The mono-national nation state re-emerged with a vengeance after the break-up of the Soviet empire in 1989. It delivered safety and security to minority groups threatened by the breakup of Yugoslavia. 'Why should I be a minority in your state when you could be a minority in mine?' became the driving logic for ethnic war and nation state formation in the ruins of Tito's Yugoslavia. The micro-states created between 1991 and 2008 – Slovenia, Croatia, Macedonia, Montenegro and Kosovo – may have been small, weak and poor by Western European standards. But they delivered two crucial security goals for people living in fear after the break-up of a coercive multinational state: deliverance from internal minorities who threatened them and protection from the territorial designs of ethnic majorities next door.

Without doubt, the bloodshed that accompanied the formation of these Balkan micro-states has given the nation state as a whole a bad name. Yet they solved the security dilemmas of vulnerable nations, and for that reason they will hold onto the allegiance of their people.

The Yugoslav experience also re-opened the painful question of the relation between state and nation for all countries where multiple nations share a single state – the United Kingdom, Spain, Canada, Belgium and the Asian and African states that contain diverse tribal and ethnic groups.

The former Yugoslavia took the road to hell, but there is another road that nation states can travel that does enable nations to share a common state. The conditions for sharing a state are at once economic, constitutional and political. What is needed is an economy sufficiently productive and prosperous to lift competing minority communities beyond a zero sum competition for resources; a constitution that outlaws tribal or ethnic favoritism in state patronage; and a democratic political system that institutionalises cross-ethnic alliance formation. Nations don't have to like each other; they can each remember a bitter past differently. On an individual level, different national groups don't necessarily need to interact or intermarry. What the multinational state must provide is a level political, economic and juridical playing field ordered by the rule of law. This is how multinational states like Canada and the

United Kingdom have managed, so far, to preserve common civic attachment to the state.

In successful multinational states their constitution, on paper and in practice, guarantees that the state is not the game preserve of the privileged or ethnically entitled few. Their legitimacy depends on constitutionally embedded respect for difference that allows different nations to live equitably under the same roof. Living together peacefully and productively is possible – but not always easy. As any family will be able to tell you, it requires authority rooted in fairness and willingness to compromise, as well as some affection among inmates. Otherwise, houses quickly turn into prisons.

There are other ways to keep multinational nation states together. China and Russia offer a model based on authoritarian state capitalism and single-party rule. These states use brute force to repress their national minorities and/or try to bribe portions of their elite. The Chechens, the Uighurs and the Tibetans all have legitimate national aspirations and all are denied legal political expression in Russia and China. In the absence of democracy or convincing forms of local self-rule, a legitimacy gap has opened up between the authoritarian state and their captive nations.

A second legitimacy gap has also opened up between state and the Russian nation. President Putin portrays himself as the authentic representative of that nation, but the urban middle class is not fooled, to judge from the massive protests that greeted his fraud-ridden re-election as president in 2012. When such a gap between state and nation opens up, propaganda and intimidation can only do so much. The regime then depends for its survival not on consent but on buying off discontent and crushing overt dissidence. Revenues from extractive industries provide the resources for Putin to manage the discontents of the nations under his control; but control depends precariously on the buoyancy of international oil and gas prices. The successful exploitation of shale gas, as well as of oil sands, which are reducing prices, could turn out to be a harbinger of regime change.

In China, too, a rising economic tide lifts enough boats to sustain the legitimacy of single-party rule, if not among the captive nations then at least among the majority Han Chinese. Freeing millions of citizens from poverty and ending the civil wars that weakened China throughout the twentieth century offer a powerful alternative narrative of legitimacy. But there is inherent instability in this growth, because it depends too much on export-oriented profit during the Long Boom, which ended in 2008. Just as in the later nineteenth century, it has proved difficult to turn that productive energy inwards from the coastal belt to benefit the mass of Chinese. Today, much abandoned half-complete construction is to be seen inland: a common sign of centrally planned failure. Moreover the pattern of coal-fired industrialisation has left a burden of pollution, which is a source of popular anger against the regime, rather as happened in the last days of Communist Eastern Europe. If the economy fails the state has only repression and divide-and-rule tactics to contain the nations that compose it.

The cohesion of multinational states that lack the rule of law and democratic pluralism will always be dependent on repression and the use of force. But even where multinational states are both lawful and democratic, their cohesion cannot be taken for granted. If economic growth fails and the state is no longer able to buy off national discontent, if the political game favours the centre at the expense of the periphery or one ethnic group at the expense of others, competition by national groups can quickly become a bitter zero-sum game. Both winners and losers in this competition can come to believe that their nation would be better off with a state of its own.

The appeal of secessionist nationalism is powerful at any time, but especially so when times are hard. Then it becomes appealing for nations to seek independence and a state that will use resources exclusively for their benefit. The resurgence of Catalan nationalism would serve as an example of these trends: a rich nation, frustrated by the cost of contributing more than its share to poorer regions of Spain, convinced that it would do better on its own and seeking a state so that Catalan nationhood can step forward and claim recognition on the international stage.

The peaceful secessionist nationalism of the Catalan, Scots or Quebecois variety is very different from the ethnic nationalism that blew the former Yugoslavia apart. Nonetheless, it repels those who believe it is better, morally and politically, for different national groups to live together under the same political roof. Those who want to move the European continent towards a federal union also look upon secessionist nationalism with especial disapproval.

Secessionist nationalism, however, won't go away simply because cosmopolitans dismiss it as atavistic or retrograde. Secessionist pressures arise whenever a nation feels its interests are no longer treated equitably by the state it shares. This political fact must be met politically, by a negotiation that leads to a constitutional settlement re-establishing the relationship between nation and state or preparing the grounds for divorce.

We are likely to see more nation states in the world, since not all existing multinational states will be able to contain secessionist pressures. Nor is it clear that supra-national organisations like the European Union actually help multinational states to contain these pressures. On the contrary, the existence of the European Union acts as a feather bed to assure nations seeking independence that they will have a soft landing should they strike out on their own. Far from extinguishing the nation state, the European Union's very existence may encourage small nations to take the secessionist road.

The European Union's impact on the nation state is complex because the ultimate purpose and destination of the Union have never been clear.

The European Union began its life in the 1950s as a limited iron and steel agreement between France and Germany, evolved into a common market, then into a currency union and now is moving towards a central bank and a common fiscal policy. The fundamental logic of the expansion has been the logic of scale: the larger the European market and the larger the population using its currency, the more powerful European states would become in the global market. While some visionaries of the European project have called for a federal Europe to replace the nation state, the actual leaders of European government have only ever endorsed enlarging the scale and power of the Union in order to strengthen their own state's leverage and power within the international system.

The European sovereign debt crisis has exposed the contradiction between the increasing powers of Brussels and the still stoutly defended prerogatives of the nation state.

The EU's common currency has encroached upon the core economic functions of the nation state: controlling the issue of money and credit and the regulation of banks and capital markets. Those who defend this federalist encroachment on economic sovereignty argue that individual nation states have little economic sovereignty left and can only preserve what they have by combining forces and pooling their resources. Those who resist the creation of a federal Europe, with a central bank and common fiscal policy, argue that these economic powers must remain within the hands of nation states precisely because the economies of each are different. Southern European economies cannot be integrated into northern ones under the same currency and fiscal regime except at an unacceptably destructive cost. Monetary and fiscal integration will weaken the sovereignty of the stronger states, while eviscerating the democracy and the economy of the weaker ones.

The travails of the European Union – and the searing debate about whether transnational pooling of sovereignty weakens or strengthens the nation state – raises in stark form the question whether the nation state is still capable of performing its fourth and most vital function: protecting citizens against the disruptive forces of the global market.

The modern state has both an enabling and protecting role in relation to the market. Domestically the state is an enabler of market operations by enforcing the rule of law, regulating competition, purchasing goods and services, managing effective demand and controlling currency and interest rates. There can be too much government intervention and too little, but there cannot be any doubt that markets cannot function efficiently without an enabling state.

Shelter from the storms

The state cannot protect citizens from their own mistakes, but it must be there to protect them from systemic risk, from those national or global economic storms that threaten their pensions, savings, investment and employment. What effective sovereignty means for an average citizen is that their state has some real, even if limited, capacity to protect them from economic harms that are not their fault. The legitimacy of democracy depends on this popular understanding of sovereignty: if we vote for politicians, they will do whatever it takes to ensure that we hold onto our jobs, our pensions and our savings.

The attachment of citizens to the nation state is intimately linked to this protective function. While patriotism is not a transaction and loyalty is not an insurance contract, both can be weakened if citizens feel their state is powerless to protect them from global storms bearing down on them from outside.

Those who criticise the European Union for its usurpation of sovereignty need to reflect on the fact that ordinary citizens, in the midst of a global economic storm, do not ask: how do I preserve my state's sovereignty? They ask instead: who will protect me best, my state alone or collective action by a group of states? The Greeks resent the usurpation of their sovereignty by European bureaucrats and yet remain convinced, by large margins, that they need to remain in the euro. Going it alone seems even worse than sticking with a common currency. They understand that sticking with a common currency means they must surrender democratic control of fiscal and monetary policy, but their need for protection trumps their concern for sovereignty.

The European Union certainly has a growing democratic deficit, but its residual legitimacy lies in meeting a need for economic protection that weak sovereigns are failing to provide. Only a Europe-wide pooling of sovereignty appears capable of providing the scale of resources needed to protect European populations from systemic risk in an open international economy. Protection, however, comes at a high political cost. Rich states resent the fact that poor ones are forcing them to pay for their mistakes, but rich ones realise that failure to assist them may drag them down too.

Pooling risk by pooling sovereignty protects the European population as a whole, but at the price of exporting moral hazard from weak states to strong ones and of transferring political responsibility out of democratic states to unelected officials.

This is not happening because of some malign plot by Brussels bureaucrats, but because four southern European nation states failed to manage their relations with global capital markets in an era of cheap credit. These states have nowhere else to turn but Europe.

The Greeks, Spaniards, Portuguese, Italians and the Irish are coming to realise that their financial and political elites have so jeopardised the sovereignty of their states that the only salvation lies in surrendering some sovereignty temporarily to outsiders. Sovereignty can be suspended on the understanding that it can be recovered when domestic political elites successfully restore control over their public finances.

The ordeal of Europe is a parable of the ordeal of the nation state in the modern global economy. The parable teaches stern lessons: nation states can only retain effective economic sovereignty if their political elites maintain fiscal and monetary discipline, do not borrow more from markets than they can repay, and maintain honest taxation regimes and credible national accounts. Their capacity to do all this, under conditions of austerity, depends on their ability to demand sacrifice and maintain equity among competing income groups. The troika, composed of the European Commission, the European Central Bank and the IMF may be exercising creditors' leverage and Europe alone may have the scale and size to provide the rescue, but only the Greek nation state has the authority to impose sacrifice upon its own people.

The travails of Europe's nation states in the global market are not exceptional. They reprise the ordeals of Latin American states in the 1980s and 1990s who ran unsustainable deficits or lost control of their currency and were forced to turn to the IMF and accept international supervision. These were, in effect, temporary suspensions of sovereignty for states unable to manage their economic relationships with the global market.

Countries like Brazil and Argentina, having endured the humiliation of suspended sovereignty twenty years ago, are now growing again and have recovered effective sovereignty.

The real issue with these suspensions of sovereign authority is that the medicine international institutions prescribe is rarely tailored to the specific needs of the country in question, as the medicine would be if it were prescribed by duly elected state authorities. The inescapable reality, however, is that international doctors are only called in when local doctors fail. Latin Americans may rail at IMF conditionality regimes as southern Europeans rail at the medicine prescribed by Brussels, but the solution is in their hands: to make fiscal responsibility and honesty about the national accounts the *sine qua non* of election to public office.

Even nation states whose leaders meet these criteria have been sorely tried by economic storms originating beyond their borders. Nation states that make up in global power for what they lack in fiscal responsibility have struggled to maintain full mastery of their own economic house. The world's most powerful sovereign, the United States, is heavily indebted to foreign holders of its Treasury bonds and the largest holder of these bonds is its chief strategic rival, China. What maintains peaceful co-dependency between these rivals is the knowledge that open economic warfare would be devastating for each. Global security – and economic prosperity – depend on these two giants understanding the depth of their interdependence as economic sovereigns.

There has always been a gulf between juridical and economic sovereignty, between the legal promise of inviolability and the constant impingement of global market forces on the sovereign state. The poor nations of Africa, Asia and Latin America have struggled since independence to deliver the mastery that juridical sovereignty promises. They have learned how hard it is for weak and poor states to deliver on that promise. What is striking now is that rich states are learning the same lesson. While they have institutions and infrastructure that poor states can only envy, they too face the continual legitimacy challenge of delivering on the promise of sovereignty, the promise that the nation state can still deliver basic economic security to its citizens.

To have and to hold

The nation state remains the political unit of choice for the world's population because it offers its citizens the core promise of politics itself: collective mastery of fate. When citizens seek to create supranational organisations like the European Union, they do so, not to supersede the nation state, but to make it capable of delivering on that promise. Globalisation has brought prosperity to billions of people, but it has deeply challenged the sovereignty of the political unit charged to master it. But to paraphrase the eighteenth-century Italian seer and philosopher Giambattista Vico, globalisation was made by people and can be understood by people, and therefore it can be controlled by people, as it always has been, through the collective political action that the nation state uniquely makes possible to us all.

– 2: The Need for Nations –

T he project of European integration, advanced by politicians and elites of defeated nations, was founded on the belief that nationhood and national self-determination were the prime causes of the wars that had ruined Europe. There were disputes as to who started it: Louis XIV? The French Revolutionaries? Napoleon? Metternich? Talleyrand? Fichte? The Revolutionaries of 1848? The Reactionaries and Monarchists? Bismarck? Garibaldi? Wagner? But, however far back you went, in the eyes of the post-war political survivors, you came across the demon of nationalism, locked in conflict with the pure spirit of Enlightenment. As a result of this founding myth European integration was conceived in one-dimensional terms, as a process of ever-increasing *unity,* under a centralised structure of command. Each increase in central power was to be matched by a diminution of national power.

In other words, the political process in Europe was endowed with a *direction*. It is not a direction that the people of Europe have chosen, and every time they are given the chance to vote they reject it – hence everything is done to ensure that they never have the chance to vote. The process moves towards centralisation, top-down control, dictatorship by unelected bureaucrats and judges, cancellation of laws passed by elected parliaments, constitutional treaties framed without any input whatsoever from the people. In the current debt crisis the European elite – composed largely of the governing circles in France and Germany – has assumed the right to depose the elected governments of Greece and Italy and to impose their own henchmen, chosen from the ranks of obedient apparatchiks. In this way, the process is moving always towards imperial government, making very clear that the opposite of the nation state is not Enlightenment but Empire. And only one thing stands opposed to this result, and that is the national sentiments of the European peoples.

As an Englishman and a lover of the civilisation of Rome I am not opposed to Empire. But it is important to recognise what it involves and to distinguish the good from the bad forms of it. In my view the good forms serve to protect local loyalties and customs under a canopy of civilisation and law; the bad forms try to extinguish local customs and rival loyalties and to replace them with a lawless and centralised power. The European Union has elements of both arrangements: but it suffers from one overwhelming defect, which is that it has never persuaded the people of Europe to accept it. Europe is, and in my view has ever been, a civilisation of nation states, founded on a specific kind of pre-political allegiance, which is the allegiance that puts territory and custom first and religion and dynasty second in the order of government. Give them a voice, therefore, and the people of Europe will express their loyalties in those terms. In so far as they have *unconditional* loyalties – loyalties that are a matter of identity rather than agreement – they take a national form.

The political class in Europe does not like this, and as a result has demonised the direct expression of national sentiments. Speak up for Jeanne d'Arc and *le pays réel*, for the 'sceptred isle' and St George, for Lemmenkäinen's gloomy forests and the 'true Finns' who roam in them, and you will be called a fascist, a racist and an extremist. There is a liturgy of denunciation here that is repeated all across Europe by a political elite that affects to despise ordinary loyalties while surreptitiously depending on them. The fact is that national sentiment is, for most ordinary Europeans, the only publicly available and publicly shared motive that will justify sacrifice in the common cause – the only source of obligation in the public sphere that is not a matter of what can be bought and sold. In so far as people do not vote to line their own pockets, it is because they also vote to protect a shared identity from the predations of those who do not belong to it, and who are attempting to pillage an inheritance to which they are not entitled. Philip Bobbitt has argued that one major effect of the wars between nation states in Europe has been the replacement of the nation state with the 'market state' – the state conceived as a firm, offering benefits in exchange for duties, which we are free to join or leave as we choose. (See *The Shield of Achilles*.) If this were true, then the nation, as an identity-forming community, would have lost its leading role in defining political choices and loyalties. Indeed, we would have emerged from the world of political loyalty altogether, into a realm of self-interested negotiations, in which sacrifices are no longer accepted, and perhaps no longer required. But if the present crisis has convinced us of nothing else, it has surely brought home to us that the capacity for sacrifice is the precondition of enduring communities, and that when the chips are down politicians both demand sacrifice and expect to receive it.

We have been made well aware by the Islamists that not everyone accepts the nation as the fount of unconditional loyalty. The followers of Sayyid Qutb tell us that national obedience is a form of idolatry, and that it is to Allah alone that obedience is owed. The European nations have never whole-heartedly accepted that kind of theocratic absolutism, and firmly rejected it at the Treaty of Westphalia. The problem for Europe is that the ensuing centuries of territorial jurisdiction have implanted sentiments that do not fit easily into any kind of imperial ambition. In the circumstances of modern democratic government it is only on behalf of the nation that people are prepared to think outside the frame of self-interest. Hence the new imperial project has entered into conflict with the only source of sentiment upon which it could conceivably draw for its legitimacy. The nation states are not equally stable, equally democratic, equally free or equally obedient to the rule of law. But they alone inspire the obedience of the European people, and without them there is no way that the machinery of the Union can act. By replacing national accountability with distant bureaucracy, that machinery has left people disarmed and bewildered in the face of the current crisis.

We see this clearly in the matter of the common currency. The euro, imposed without proof that the people of the 'Eurozone' had any desire for it, was immediately understood, by many politicians in the Mediterranean, as a way of enlarging the national debt. This was very obviously the case in Greece. Bonds issued in euros would benefit from the strength and probity of the northern economies, and would be regarded as safe bets by investors who would not dream of buying bonds issued in drachmas. And the people of Greece agreed, since nobody alerted them to the cost – the *national* cost – that will be paid, once the Eurozone breaks up, as surely it must. Now that the day of reckoning is approaching, people all across the continent sense the need to prepare themselves for hard times. In a crisis people 'take stock', which means that they retreat to the primary source of their social attachment, and prepare to defend it. They do not do this consciously. But they do it nevertheless, and the futile attempt by the politicians to denounce the 'extremism' of the people whose inheritance they have squandered merely exacerbates the reaction. But the situation is not a happy one, since there is no trans-national idea of Europe to which the politician can appeal by way of identifying an object of loyalty outside the borders of the nation state. The half-century of peace and prosperity has fed upon the European cultural inheritance without renewing it. For it is all but impossible for a European politician to evoke the civilisation of Europe when its source – the Christian Religion – has been expunged from official documents and openly repudiated by the European courts. One ground of the current attacks on the 'nationalist' government of Hungary by the European Commission is that the Hungarians have drawn up a constitution which, in its preamble, describes the Hungarians as a 'Christian nation': two words that have been purged from the official vocabulary of Europe.

Indeed, the European process, because it is committed to denying the validity of national cultures, also denies the validity of the European cultural inheritance upon which they draw. The constitutional treaties and trans-national courts have made a point of granting no favours to the Christian faith or to the morality that has sprung from it. A 'cult of the minority' has been imposed from above, as a kind of rebuke to the people of Europe for being Europeans in spirit. This official multiculturalism has done nothing to reconcile immigrant communities to their new surroundings; instead it has destroyed much that was confident and joyful in the national cultures of Europe and rejected the Christian pieties in favour of a kind of morose materialism.

The result of official multiculturalism is in fact cultural blindness – an inability to perceive the real cultural distinctions that obtain across the European continent and which are rooted in the custom and history of the nation states. If the architects of the euro had taken national cultures properly into account they would have known that the effect of imposing a single currency on Greece and Germany would be to encourage Greece to transfer its debts to Germany, on the understanding that the further away the creditor the less the obligation to repay. They would have recognised that laws, obligations, and sovereignty don't have quite the same meaning in the Mediterranean as they do on the Baltic, and that in a society used to kleptocratic government the fairest way out of an economic crisis is by devaluation – in other words, by stealing equally from everybody.

Why didn't the architects of the euro know those things? The answer is to be found deep within the European project. Cultural facts were simply *impalpable* to the Eurocrats. Allowing themselves to perceive culture would be tantamount to recognising that their project was an impossible one. This would have mattered less if they had another project with which to replace it. But – like all radical projects – that of the European Union was conceived without a Plan B. Hence it is destined to collapse and, in the course of its collapse, to drag our continent down. An enormous pool of pretence has accumulated at the centre of the project, while the political class skirmishes at the edges, in an attempt to fend off the constant assaults of reality.

Thus we have to pretend that the long observed distinctions between the Protestant north of our continent and the Catholic and Orthodox south is of no economic significance. Being a cultural fact it is unperceivable, notwithstanding Weber's (admittedly exaggerated) attempt to make it central to economic history. The difference between the culture of common law and that of the *code Napoléon* has likewise been ignored, at the cost of alienating the British and the northern Europeans, for whom law has ever been a social rather than a political product. The distinction between the Roman and the Ottoman legal legacies has been set aside, as has that between countries where law is certain and judges incorruptible and places where law is only the last resort in a system of bribes. Times and speeds of work, and the balance between work and leisure, which go to the heart of every community since they define its relation to time, are ignored, or else regimented by a futile edict from the centre. And everything is to be brought into line by those frightening courts – the European Court of Justice and the European Court of Human Rights – whose unelected judges never pay the cost of their decisions, and whose agenda of 'ever-closer union' and 'non-discrimination' is calculated to wipe away the traces of local loyalties, family-based morality, and rooted ways of life. Not surprisingly, when you build an empire on such massive pretences, it very soon becomes unstable.

We can rescue Europe, it seems to me, only if we can recover the project that Charles de Gaulle wished to place at its heart, and which was effectively scotched by Jean Monnet – the project of a Europe of Nations. It will not be easy to unravel the web of regulations and edicts contained in the 170,000 pages of the *acquis communautaire*; nor will it be easy to redefine the roles and the structures of the European courts and the competences of the European Institutions. But the most difficult thing will be to obtain agreement on what national sovereignty really means. In particular, what will sovereignty mean in the aftermath of the European Union? Conservative politicians in Britain often speak of recapturing powers from Brussels, as though these powers will not have been altered by captivity, and as though they can be easily domesticated when they are brought back home. This is like Menelaus thinking that home life in Mycenae would be just the same when he had returned victorious from Troy, the recaptured Helen obediently trotting behind, as it was in the good old days before she left.

The situation of Europe today reminds us that by conceiving pre-political loyalties in national rather than religious terms, European civilisation has made room for the Enlightenment. The national idea is not the enemy of Enlightenment but its necessary precondition. National loyalty marginalises loyalties of family, tribe and faith, and places before the citizen's eyes, as the focus of his patriotic feeling, not a person or a group but a country. This country is defined by a territory, and by the history, culture and law that have made that territory *ours*. It is the emergence of territory from behind religion, tribe and dynasty that characterises the nationalist art and literature of the nineteenth century, and the national anthems of the self-identifying nations were conceived as invocations of home, in the manner of Sibelius's *Finlandia* or our own unofficial national anthem, 'Land of Hope and Glory'.

In short, Enlightenment means borders. Take away borders, and people begin to identify themselves not by territory and law, but by tribe, race or religion. Nationality is composed of land, together with the narrative of its possession. It is this form of territorial loyalty that has enabled people in Western democracies to exist side by side, respecting each other's rights as citizens, despite radical differences in faith, and without any bonds of family, kinship or long-term local custom to sustain the solidarity between them. For on the foundation of territorial attachment it has been possible to build a kind of civic patriotism, which acknowledges institutions and laws as shared possessions, and which can extend a welcome to those who have entered the social contract from outside. You cannot immigrate into a tribe, a family or a faith; but you can immigrate into a country, provided you are prepared to obey the rules that make that country into a home.

National loyalty is not known everywhere in the world. Consider Somalia. People sometimes refer to Somalia as a 'failed state', since it has no central government capable of making decisions on behalf of the people as a whole, or of imposing any kind of legal order. But the real trouble with Somalia is that it is a failed nation. It has never developed the kind of secular, territorial and law-minded sovereignty that makes it possible for a country to shape itself as a nation state rather than an assemblage of competing tribes and families.

This observation is, of course, pertinent to the Middle East as a whole today, where we find the remnants of a great Islamic Empire divided into nation states. With a few exceptions this division is the result of boundaries drawn on the map by Western powers, and notably by Britain and France as a result of the Sykes-Picot accords of 1917. But the vexed question of Islam and modernity would take us too far from our topic; suffice it to say that tribe and creed have always been more important than sovereignty in Islamic ways of thinking, and the non-emergence of nations in the Middle East is partly explained by this, as is their embryonic emergence in those countries, like Lebanon and Egypt, with substantial Christian minorities, maintaining long-standing trade links with Europe.

I have no doubt that it is the long centuries of Christian dominance in Europe which laid the foundations of national loyalty, as a loyalty above those of faith and family, and on which a secular jurisdiction and an order of citizenship can be founded. It may sound paradoxical, to identify a religion as the major force behind the development of secular government. But we should remember the peculiar circumstances in which Christianity entered the world. The Jews were a closed community, bound in a tight web of religious legalisms, but governed from Rome by a law which made no reference to any God and which offered an ideal of citizenship to which every free subject of the Empire might aspire.

Christ found himself in conflict with the legalism of his fellow Jews, and in broad sympathy with the idea of secular government – hence his famous words in the parable of the Tribute Money: render unto Caesar what is Caesar's and to God what is God's. The Christian faith was shaped by St Paul for the use of communities within the Empire, who wanted only space to pursue their worship, and had no intention of challenging the secular powers. Hence 'the powers that be are ordained of God' (Romans 13). And this idea of dual loyalty continued after Constantine, being endorsed by Pope Gelasius the First in the sixth century, in his doctrine of the two swords given to mankind for their government, that which guards the body politic, and that which guards the individual soul. It is this deep endorsement of secular law by the early Church that was responsible for the subsequent developments in Europe – through the Reformation and the Enlightenment – to the purely territorial law that prevails in the West today.

It is very clear from the history of our continent, that new forms of solidarity have here come into being which owe much to the Christian inheritance, but which are premised on the assumption that legitimacy is a man-made and not a God-bestowed achievement. Nations emerged as forms of pre-political order that contain within themselves the principles that would legitimise sovereign government. Political theorists of the Enlightenment such as Locke and Rousseau tried to encapsulate this legitimising process in a social contract, by which the members of society form an agreement to be governed in a certain way in exchange for renouncing the state of nature. But it is surely obvious that if people assemble to consider a contract that will unite them, it is because they already belong together, already acknowledge that the welfare of each depends upon the actions of all. A contract, however strong its terms, can never establish more than a *conditional* obligation, whereas political order depends, in the end, on an unconditional component, as do marriage and the family. Without this unconditional component no community can survive a real crisis.

The social contract therefore establishes a form of government that will protect and perpetuate an allegiance that precedes the contract and makes it possible. This allegiance is shaped by history and territory, and by all the forms of association that spring from these, notably language, customary law and religious observance. Seeing things in this way, religious observance is demoted to one factor among others, and is reshaped as a *subject* of law, rather than a source of it. That, to my mind, is the great achievement of European civilisation: to have placed man-made law at the heart of the community, to have subordinated all associations, including those stemming from religion, to the demands of the secular jurisdiction, and to have established the institutions through which law can adapt to changes in social life instead of blurting out some 'eternal' message revealed in circumstances that have vanished, leaving no other trace.

However, law so conceived is territorial and therefore national. It is a law that defines boundaries, beyond which its writ does not run. Claims to jurisdiction from a place outside those boundaries are fiercely resisted, as we know from the history of England and from the conflict between the crown and the papacy that has been decisive in forming many of the nation states of Europe. When it is proposed that the *Corpus Juris,* the EU's foray into establishing European criminal law, should permit European courts to charge British citizens with criminal offences and extradite them to the place most convenient for their trial, it is hardly surprising that British people receive this suggestion with outrage. Their conception of law is the common law conception, which does not permit people to be held indefinitely without trial, and which depends for its authority on the 'law of the land', as embodied in cases decided in the sovereign territory of the English Crown. This attachment of law to territory is not some arbitrary limitation, as though there were a universal jurisdiction from which local jurisdictions are derived by restriction. It is the very essence of law, as the European experience has defined it. We are heirs to a conception of law as arising from the attempt to settle conflicts, to establish institutions, to adjudicate rights and duties, among people who are bound to each other as neighbours. Law, as we know it, is produced by the place that needed it, and is marked by the history of that place. (The contrast with the *Shari'ah* is obvious, as is the contrast with the 'natural law' of the stoics and the Universal Church.)

Hence the attempt to build a European Empire of laws that depend upon no national allegiance for their authority is not merely bound to fail. It is likely also to undermine the authority of secular law in the minds of the European people. There is already in the social contract theories of the eighteenth century a kind of wishful thinking about human nature, a belief that people can reshape all their obligations without reference to their affections, so as to produce an abstract calculus of rights and duties in the place of their contingent and historical ties. The French revolutionaries began their seizure of power in this way, proposing a declaration of the rights of man and the citizen that would sweep away all the arbitrary arrangements of history and place Reason on the throne that had previously been occupied by a mere human being, who had arrived there by the accident of succession. But within weeks of the Declaration the country was being governed in the name of the Nation, the *Patrie*, and the old contingent association was being summoned in another and (to my mind) far more dangerous form, in order to fill the gap in people's affections that had been made by the destruction of customary loyalty, religious usage, and the unquestioned ways of neighbourhood. This was clearly perceived by Burke, who reminded his readers that human beings are thrown together by accidents that they do not choose, and derive their affections not from their decisions but from their circumstances. It is proximity, not reason, that is the foundation of ordinary charitable feeling. Take that thought seriously, and you quickly come to see that territorial forms of association are the best remedy that we have against the divisive call of ideology. National attachment is precisely what prevents 'extremism' from taking hold of the ordinary conscience.

Nationalism is an ideological attempt to *supplant* customary and neighbourly loyalties with something more like a religious loyalty – a loyalty based on doctrine and commitment. Ordinary national loyalty, by contrast, is the by-product of settlement. It comes about because people have ways of resolving their disputes, ways of getting together, ways of cooperating, ways of celebrating and worshipping that seal the bond between them without ever making that bond explicit as a doctrine. This is surely how ordinary people live, and it is at the root of all that is best in human society, namely that we are attached to what goes on around us, grow together with it, and learn the ways of peaceful association as *our* ways, which are right because they are ours and because they unite us with those who came before us and those for whom we will in turn make way. Seen in that way national feelings are not just natural, they are essentially *legitimising*. They call upon the sources of social affection, and bestow that affection on customs that have proved their worth over time, by enabling a community to settle its disputes and achieve equilibrium in the changing circumstances of life.

National sentiments enable people successfully to defend themselves in wartime. But they are also essential in peacetime too. This we are now seeing in Europe, as the sovereign debt crisis begins to affect the lives of ordinary people. Governments are calling on their citizens to make sacrifices for the common good. They are not asking them to make sacrifices for 'Europe', still less for the European Union. If they were to use this language then they would be forced to recognise that Europe is not the bureaucratic machine which has conferred upon them the small measure of legitimacy that they can claim, but a spiritual inheritance that the machine has tried to extirpate. Hence the only invocations that they can make address national sentiments.

They speak of the need to pull together, for the sake of *our* community, and at every point their language invokes the contingencies of human affection that make it possible for people to give up something for the sake of others – a habit of mind that social democracies do not normally encourage. They are not speaking the language of nationalism, but the language of attachment, which is something entirely different. Their response to the crisis of Europe reveals that the nation state is not the problem but the solution – it contains within itself the only motives to which politicians can now appeal, when the effects of the European project are finally being felt across the continent.

Part II
Breaking Up or Sticking Together

Jean Bethke Elshtain

– 3: Must We Really Hang Together or Hang Separately? –

We are in a drawn-out period of change in national and international governance. Those driving change, or commenting from the sidelines, have wildly differing viewpoints, but broadly speaking fall into two camps.

On the one hand we have those I call the 'new utopians', who insist that the state is the serpent in the garden, poisoning any hope for a bright new day of global citizenship and international conflict resolution. On the other hand, we find defenders of the state, who underscore a point made sixty years ago by the political philosopher Hannah Arendt, insisting that civic identity is meaningful only within a secure, ordered, circumscribed political space in which citizens can act together: the state. I am in the latter camp. I believe that the modern nation state, especially in its constitutional form is a great historic achievement. It offered and offers the best alternative, in a diverse, plural and fractious world, to internecine warfare and the phenomenon we now call the 'failed state'.

There is a vitally important difference that we must consider when discussing the modern nation state, namely, is it a pure nation state, or a constitutional state also allowing for a civic, rather than national form of adherence? In addition to those born into it, a constitutional state is also open to all those born elsewhere who seek civic identity and go through a process of 'naturalisation' to enter into full civic membership if these others come from elsewhere. In the case of a pure nation state, problems arise when the geographical boundaries of the designated nation do not match precisely with traditional territorial boundaries. The grievance then becomes a 'minorities' problem: some on the state territory are the 'wrong' ethnicity, so do they really belong?

Because it has become the dominant form, my focus will be on the modern civic state, a constitutional state that has been the vehicle of civic identity for a particular nation or people historically. This existing civic identity does not prevent others becoming full-fledged co-equal citizens today, even though they might not share fully the ethnic, linguistic, and cultural markers of that state's historic life. I do not deny the problem of embedded (or stimulated) irreconcilabilities that descend into civil war. Nor am I unaware of the extreme anxiety and fear that such 'Balkanisation' engenders and the degree to which they have fed and still feed antipathy to the concept of the state. But mainly I care about the less noticed but larger case, where multiple allegiances work. So for that reason, as a theologian, I shall explore these questions in an unexpected but I hope helpful fashion.

Why should states stick together even though there may be strong, identifiable cultural and other differences between significant portions of their populations? What is the problem with becoming a microstate serving as the vehicle of a single nation, such as for example the Spanish regions, or the constituent parts of Great Britain? Or, taking a different path, what is the problem with permitting more and more of one's civic life to be overtaken by 'global governance', by international bodies that make key, often grave, decisions for a number of bodies politic without the deliberate consent or dissent of the citizens of those polities?

To reflect on shared civic membership despite strong differences in fundamental orientations and identities, let us not turn to a review of substantive case studies but to a treatment of an underlying principle. Let us turn to St Augustine and his magisterial treatment of political issues in *The City of God*. In a nutshell, his argument is that Christians are, indeed, members of the earthly city. But they are members with a difference: their eyes are fixed on the heavenly city; that is the way their love is ordered. So does that mean that they can only have social, political, and cultural relations with their own group of fellow confessing Christians in the earthly city?

Not at all. Indeed, Augustine strives with considerable aplomb to sketch out what Christians share with their fellow citizens; why, therefore, they have a stake in the fate of their earthly polity even though it is by no means a Christian state. Remember that Augustine, almost alone among his contemporaries, resisted the siren song of the notion of a 'Christian empire'. He had been tempted but he resisted, seeking to avoid an idolatry of earthly power by mapping it directly onto the heavenly city, collapsing thereby the here-and-now and the final, heaven-like end-state of history or 'eschaton'. There is always an eschatological gap for Augustine. It is simply the fact of the matter. The factual reality is that one lives in a world in which Christians are a minority. They may always remain so. On what terms does this minority share civic life with others?

All persons, Christian and non-Christian, have a stake in the peace, order, and justice of the earthly city. All have a stake in helping to sustain a world in which the multiple institutions of society, beginning with the family, are instruments of justice and a righteous order, ideally forming a *tranquillitas ordinis* – a grounded peace. The Gospel calls Christians to love their neighbour towards whom they bear obligations. A political body can only fulfill its God-given obligations and functions if it is authoritative enough to maintain order and justice. At the same time, it has to desist from going down the pathway of the disorder of unjust Empire or some similar route (here, as in other places, Augustine acknowledges the beneficial fruits of Roman rule). He just wants us to consider the scale and frequency of wars and all the blood that was shed. Hopefully, one can scale down such temporal ambition and attain those earthly achievable goals of a measure of justice, order, and peace without the overweening domination of authoritarian orders built upon a lust to dominate, the *libido dominandi*. This lust for domination exists in each and every one of us. It exemplifies our fall from grace and, thus, our fallen world far away from paradise.

Let's jump ahead from late antiquity to the triumph of the modern state. In the Reformation Era, theologians argued for an ideal: for a sovereign state whose authority should be limited by law. This point had been strongly underwritten by St Thomas Aquinas in his discourse on the limits to the power of the king, lest he transmogrify into a tyrant. Robin Lovin, a political theologian writing today, highlights this singular accomplishment which the Reformation contributed to: 'The successful modern state, designed by people who were seeking peace and order, thus provides a setting in which they can pursue goods that are more abundant and complex than the need for security, taken by itself, would suggest. Indeed, where the modern state is working well, people may hardly think about security at all, as they open the castle gates, landscape their moats, go about their business on the highways, and draw up legal documents that lock in their expectation of future gain.'[1]

Historically, a concern for security and order helped to create the political preconditions for much else besides. That 'much else besides' cannot be realised in a world in which each distinct, identifiable 'minority' group hives itself off from the political body – or is excluded through force. Why not? Because it is difficult if not impossible to achieve and to sustain the preconditions of security and order for 'much else besides' if one is a small, relatively powerless, hence vulnerable 'micro-state'. Such relatively weak entities constitute an ever-present temptation to the more powerful to absorb and to subdue them. In our rush nowadays to 'celebrate diversity' we tend to forget the story of that diversity as it was enacted when the nationality principle triumphed as the basis for state formation and civic membership.

This brings us to an era strongly on my mind, namely post-World War One Europe. The principle of national self-determination set in motion the break-up of conglomerate bodies like the Austro-Hungarian Empire on the premise that such entities violated that newly regnant principle. For architects of national self-determination like American President Woodrow Wilson, violation of national self-determination was not simply a political but a moral issue. It was wrong to occlude the separate identities and aspirations of distinct peoples, of diverse nationalities. He imagined a far more pacific world to follow, having set upon nationality as the irritant in the image that is a primary occasion for international conflict.

Whenever this logic is applied the vexing matter of difference arises. You simply cannot map the nationality principle perfectly onto a territorial entity. There are always some who do not fit. Their relationship to the new state is to be governed by settled treaties that clarify their status and solidify their 'right' to be within a state that is seen, quite explicitly, as the vehicle of previously suppressed national aspirations. One could imagine this working itself out in relatively benign ways. But the seeds are sown for the pernicious conclusion that 'others ought to be elsewhere': they do not belong; they do not fit; they cannot be part of the nation state, with the emphasis on 'nation'. As we consider the fruits of national self-determination in the inter-war period, it was, after all, the status of an ethnic minority tucked within the body of the Czechoslovakian state – the Sudetenland Germans – that became the occasion for Hitler's policy of aggressive war.

Since the debacles of the First and Second World Wars, this sort of ethnic fragmentation of political bodies has been called 'balkanisation'. It has become one worst-case scenario that is often pitted against another worst-case scenario, namely, some sort of homogenised imposition of political rule, as if these were the only available alternatives in the world as we know it. In practice, what came into being, in the United States, as well as in other places, was a reasonably well functioning civic state consisting of a mix of nationalities. In the case of the United States, immigration in the last decades of the nineteenth century and early decades of the twentieth had been quite simply staggering. My own maternal grandparents, ethnic Germans living in Russia, made their way to the United States in this period. They entered into civic membership under the presupposition that what was to be shared – the necessary glue to hold the polity together – was the commitment to the constitutive constitutional principles that afforded the framework of the United States in the first instance. This was a polity based on shared presuppositions and not shared ethnicity.

It didn't work out so smoothly, of course. Superordinate and subordinate groups were established on the basis of who got here first and who best represented and defined a modern democracy. But the overriding issue, namely, that there was a race of people in the US that did not fully fit, that could never achieve full civic status, first invited a terrible Civil War that cost 650,000 casualties. Second, it provoked a major civic crisis in the twentieth century in order to realise more completely the promises and premises put in place at the conclusion of America's most bloody conflict.

President Abraham Lincoln's argument throughout the American Civil War had been that the unity of America, her ongoing existence within the framework of the constitution, was the superordinate good at stake. There are many today who criticise Lincoln for that: he should have put slavery first, should have fought to extirpate it even though the heavens might fall and the Union crash to bits. Lincoln saw it quite differently, almost mystically. The hard-headed practical point, he insisted, was that it required the ongoing existence of an ordered polity, the United States of America, to provide the space within which the evil of slavery could finally be brought to an end and slaves finally made full-fledged citizens. Lincoln was not starry-eyed about social equality. It was full civic membership he had in mind – that and the eradication of the categories of race and ethnicity as the basis for that membership.

In our present moment cherishing pluralism and diversity, such celebration has lent credence to many claims for independent 'sovereignties' based on the old national principles. For some, this is a happy thing: it invites proper recognition for those who have been subordinated, whose identities have been submerged, within the wider political body in which they are nested. For others, it is a recipe for disaster as the category of 'difference' can quite easily morph into one of 'division' – and dangerous division at that. One can readily take the point of catalogued historic grievances: the principle of unity or commonality demanded too much homogeneity and this 'too much' effaced the distinctiveness of particular communities. Oddly enough, the 'solution' proposed is one that requires strong unity, as nationality and civic identity should now closely mesh.

Even as such contestations trudge forward – one thinks for example of Quebec separatism or the Scottish independence movement – philosophic arguments as to what actually constitutes the human common good are being mounted. Citizens in the modern West face nothing less than a contestation between competing comprehensive visions of the profane and the sacred. In this contestation some visions must give way – give ground – to others. Thus, the modern secular state cannot tolerate a full-blown 'religious' comprehensive understanding to trump at any turn the secular state's vision of the human good. The one – religion – must be evaluated from the point of view of the other – the state. For religion presages dangerous division whereas the state promises comity in so far as there are limits to how much diversity is permitted in order for competing articulations of a comprehensive good to co-exist.

How does one distinguish between imposed unity and the relatively amicable sharing implied by the notion of overlapping consensus? How 'thick' must agreement be about the human good? In Lovin's words: 'How "thin" can the good be that all share before they share nothing but their disagreements about the good? How much conflict over these questions can a community handle, not in the occasional crisis, but as an ongoing part of ordinary public life?'[2] The fond hope is that even as goods conflict they also overlap, that there are fundamental principles around which a civic identity can successfully cluster. Suffice to say that it can only work if there is also agreement on which vision of the comprehensive good trumps in cases of irreconcilable conflict.

The alternative to overlapping consensus is usually called *modus vivendi*: there is no presupposition of deep sharing or widespread overlapping consensus. But there is an agreement on 'live and let live' – you have your values; I have mine and we duke it out inside the space the state affords us. Nothing more, presumably, is required to bind us together; to 'cohere' us for the purpose of maintaining the continuity of the state and providing for our security and for civic order.

In the most magisterial articulations of the national principle, one finds a homeland bound by so much – historic ties, shared language, shared culture, especially religious faith, ancient customs and laws. The liberal constitutional ideal of overlapping consensus sounds awfully abstract, remote and legalistic by contrast. And compared to that, the modus vivendi is even 'thinner' yet. Plus, modus vivendi appears to turn the state into nothing more than a convenience store. 'I play the game so long as I get a good bit of what I want out of it. I follow the rules because they give me that possibility.' There is no grandeur in such a vision, to put it mildly. Unfortunately, the old national principle is, for the most part, unavailable as a reference. That sort of thickness of identity flies in the face of the conditions of late modernity. But it is not entirely beyond reach and lingers as a way to name an aspiration and a past reality, no doubt one viewed through rose-coloured spectacles.

How 'thick' does our sharing have to be? I don't think we really know for sure. But there must be civic glue that goes beyond economic self-interest. Personal gain is a principle that can take us anywhere that we might find economic reward, indifferent, indeed, to which polity that might happen to be. Can the sharing of a commitment to creating and sustaining this civic space provide what is needed over time? In a way, that is the premise of constitutionalism: one coheres through one's adherence to the constitutive principles of the polity. More may be desired – the sharing of songs, symbols, pledges, stories – and that will surely follow upon committing oneself to the ongoing life and well-being of a polity over time. Demanding more as the price paid for membership is likely to invite those reactions that we call 'separatism' – because the 'thickness' being proclaimed seems to possibly exclude me and my group and its history. Ironically, then, in trying to seal a civic identity for all through a strong principle of national cohesion we may set in motion a clamor for difference that undermines our fondest dreams of unity.

So what are our 'real' possibilities? Let's put this as positively as we can because, as I stated at the outset, the achievement of a stable, functioning state is a considerable one that we all should be grateful for. Our modern variants of the civic state are probably some messy combination of remembered portions of 'nationhood' in the older sense, of partial articulations of a comprehensive good, of modus vivendi and of a strong commitment to the constitutive principles that help such pluralities to inhabit a shared space. At its best, the modern civic state affords people a world in which they can go about their business, raise their families, worship God as their consciences dictate, educate their children according to their own lights, at least in a significant part, rather than just the state's, and so on.

We cannot measure 'our need for the modern state' by 'the quality of our theories about it but, rather, by what it does that no other institution can do. We lack institutions with global scope that are capable of providing order, including provision for the enforcement of whatever human rights our substantive theories of the human good tell us people ought to have.'[3]

The state is a political entity that exercises responsibility for those within its borders. It can be called to account if it fails miserably in those responsibilities, whether out of internal weakness (failed states, often failed because of incessant interminable internal conflict) or knowing and explicit malfeasance (committing genocide against one segment of its own population.) The state principle of sovereignty once insulated states from such challenges. The irony of the present moment resides in the very success of the state – the greater its transparency and accountability, the more it can be held to account. We have no other institution to do this. We simply do not know how to create anything else that could be turned into the basis for a global order. This does not, of course, preclude international NGOs from doing their work, interest groups functioning across state borders and trans-national church bodies carrying out their vital work in many areas.

9/11, that terrible day, reminded Americans of what states are for. At rock bottom, they are to prevent a Hobbesian nightmare. They are to forestall violent and premature death. Most of the time we need not think about that, at least not those of us who hail from the West within which the state principle has been most fully and securely realised. Others have not been so lucky. No wonder they want states. They worry considerably less about competing theories of the state. Instead they focus on how to get a viable political body up and running, how to stabilise it and how to help to ensure its continuity in its existing geographical boundaries. Only a cohesive state affords citizens the spaces within which they live and work and may even flourish.

Notes

1 Lovin, R., *Christian Realism and the New Realities* (2008; Cambridge: Cambridge University Press), p.270.
2 Ibid., p.111.
3 Ibid., p. 159, here characterising the position he associates with Elshtain and other 'Anti-utopian Realists'.

Daniel Hannan

– 2: The Right to Secede –

When a *bien pensant* Europhile wishes to signal his strongest possible disapproval of something, he will use one of two words: 'nationalist' or 'populist'. Both epithets have become somewhat detached from their literal meanings. To adapt George Orwell on the word 'fascist', they have now little meaning except in so far as they signify 'something not desirable'. It is nonetheless interesting to see the two words so often yoked together, for they both carry a democratic implication. For example, any referendum that results in a rejection of closer European integration (which is to say, almost every referendum on the subject) is dismissed as both nationalist and populist. Any politician who accepts the result of such a poll is given both soubriquets in an especially bellicose tone. They are indeed linked concepts. As Charles de Gaulle put it in 1942: 'Democracy for me perfectly matches national sovereignty. Democracy is the government of the people by the people, and national sovereignty is the people exercising their sovereign right without restriction.'*

* '*La démocratie se confond exactement, pour moi, avec la souveraineté nationale. La démocratie c'est le gouvernement du peuple par le peuple, et la souveraineté nationale, c'est le peuple exerçant sa souveraineté sans entrave.*'

Nowadays, that notion sounds a little archaic; but in 1942, it would have seemed obvious. Democracy in its modern form had always been linked to the national principle. When radicals in the eighteenth and nineteenth centuries began to argue for one-man-one-vote, they almost invariably found themselves challenging the existing multinational units that existed across Europe. Having posited the revolutionary idea that government should be carried out by and for the people, they found that they had immediately raised another question: what people? Within what unit, in other words, were these democratic arguments to be played out? That question had only one possible answer, and the democrats found it at once. Representative government, they argued, would work best within a population whose members felt enough in common one with another to accept government from each other's hands: in other words, within a nation. As the Italian patriot Giuseppe Mazzini put it, in perhaps the pithiest ever statement of the case for self-determination: 'Where there is a nation, let there be a state'.

A community of identity might rest on many things: history, geography, culture or religion. Language is the most common basis for nationhood, but there are exceptions. A strong sense of national identity can exist in a multilingual territory (Switzerland, for example); conversely, a monolingual territory might contain more than one national identity (as among the Serbo-Croat speakers of the former Yugoslavia or the

English speakers of the British Isles). It is important to stress at the outset that these things are rarely straight-forward. People are capable of sustaining more than one identity: you might feel Scottish as well as British, Corsican as well as French. These identities can mutate over time. An arbitrary political frontier might, as the decades pass, become a genuine national one (some-thing of the sort has happened between Austria and southern Germany, and across much of South Ameri-ca). And, of course, languages themselves are political. When, following devolution, Irish was recognised as an official language in Northern Ireland (despite not be-ing the native tongue of anyone born there), Unionists responded by granting equal status to 'Ulster Scots' – which until then had been generally considered a pat-ois. As the Yiddish linguist Max Weinreich observed, 'a language is a dialect with an army and navy'. None of these complications, though, compromises the es-sential principle. A polity functions best when there is a sense of shared identity. That sense, being visceral, might defy logical definition; but it is no less real for that.

Multinational democracies are rarely stable. By multinational, I don't mean a society which is in the process of assimilating minorities, nor yet one with small foreign populations. Virtually every state in the world has some minorities, if only as the result of im-migration. I am talking here of states where large and settled communities have different loyalties. Many such states have existed through history, but they have rarely been democratic. Indeed, the rule is that, once their peoples are given the vote, they opt for separation. The Soviet and Yugoslav federations went the same way as the Ottoman and Habsburg empires: their constituent peoples couldn't be held together once they were free to choose.

To repeat, these things are rarely clear-cut. A multinational democracy can unravel slowly and peacefully, as Belgium has been doing for decades. It can tolerate a measure of continuing secessionist discontent without ceasing to be democratic, as India does. And, of course, not all separatist feelings are of equal intensity. Let us take two examples, one from either end of the spectrum. The world's newest state, South Sudan, was different in almost every way from the rest of Sudan: racially, religiously, linguistically. It had been through a secessionist war, and eventually broke away in rancour and enmity. No one, by contrast, has ever fired a shot in anger over the issue of Scottish secession. Indeed, it is far from clear that Scottish identity is of the kind that generally constitutes national separateness. On most of the usual denominators, Scotland forms part of the same national continuum as the rest of the United Kingdom. Its people watch the same television programmes, follow the same sports, eat the same food, shop at the same chains and speak the same language as those elsewhere in Britain. As the aboriginal Unionist, James VI & I, put it: 'Hath not God first united these Kingdoms, both in Language and in Religion and in Similitude of Manners? Hath He not made us all in one Island, compassed by one Sea?' Opinion polls in Scotland suggest that the issue of independence turns mainly on the economics. A survey by Scottish Social Attitudes in December 2011 found that, if separation would make then £500 a year better off, Scots would back it by 65 per cent to 25; told that it would make them £500 a year worse off, only 21 per cent supported it, with 66 per cent opposed. It is hard to believe that any such considerations would have swayed the people of South Sudan, who voted by 98 per cent in a referendum for secession. Unlike Scots, they were in no doubt that they constituted a wholly separate people from their neighbours.

For all these shades of grey, the principle holds. Other things being equal, our inclination should be to allow people to determine their own borders. Or, to put it another way, the most important consideration when determining national frontiers should be the wishes of the inhabitants. This is not to say that alternative claims – geography, history, past treaties, rights of the residual state to access – have no force; simply that they ought not to override the claim of self-determination. This point is worth emphasising because, at present, our ruling ideology is based on precisely the opposite principle. International organisations – naturally enough, you might say – actively *oppose* the national principle. The UN and the EU, in particular, hold up the multinational state as an end in itself, and are prepared to invest considerable resources in ensuring that state borders don't coincide with ethnographic ones. The publicly stated reason is that it would condone and encourage visceral hatred at best and ethnic cleansing at worst. This is most obvious in the case of the two European territories that the international community administers as protectorates: Bosnia-Herzegovina and Kosovo. The former is run by an EU-appointed High Representative, the latter remained until very recently under the exclusive auspices of a UN-approved Special Representative. There are publicly stated reasons for insisting on misalignments between borders and people. In both cases, the primary purpose of such rule is to prevent a readjustment of borders along the lines that local people would favour.

In neither case is the territorial integrity of the state based on a fear of ethnic cleansing. On the contrary, the Serbs of both territories are now clustered conveniently close to Serbia proper. In the case of Kosovo, the de facto border is already the ethnographic one. But to regularise this line would mean accepting the validity of national self-determination as a concept, which would, of course, destroy the intellectual foundations of the entire European project. As Upton Sinclair used to observe, it is remarkably difficult to make a man understand something when his salary depends upon his not understanding it. And so, in pursuit of multi-nationalism, democracy is vitiated. Dozens of elected officials have been dismissed in Bosnia-Herzegovina for, in effect, failing to uphold the EU's approved orthodoxy of multinationalism. Both states have adopted variants of the EU flag, so as to emphasise their post-national nature. Kosovo's first national anthem was the EU's own 'Ode to Joy'. When it eventually wrote its own, it plumped for a wordless tune called 'Europe'.

In other words, the EU is exporting its ideology. It is determined to ensure that neighbouring countries form political units based on something other than the national principle. Why? Because European construction itself rests on the idea that national loyalties are arbitrary, transient and discreditable. When it bars the election of nationalist politicians in its satrapies, it is simply extending the principle that leads it to disallow 'no' votes in referendums within its own borders. De Gaulle was right to say that democracy and national self-determination are the same thing. Deny the second and, pretty soon, you find yourself having to deny the first.

While on the subject of the Balkans, it's worth dealing with one of the more common objections to the right of self-determination, namely the idea that partition is invariably a wretched and violent experience. It can be, of course. Any change in political borders is potentially disruptive. In British India, partition resulted in terror and bloodshed, and in repeated wars between India and Pakistan. In Ireland (or, strictly speaking, in the United Kingdom, which was the entity partitioned in 1921), the new frontier inflamed tensions. There were civil wars on both sides of it: a short and intense one to the south, a protracted and intermittent one to the north.In both cases, though, it can at least be argued that these problems were greatly exacerbated by a failure properly to apply the national principle. The treaty, which established Northern Ireland also provided for a Boundary Commission to redraw the border. It met between 1922 and 1925 and duly recommended substantial changes: the Irish Free State would have gained South Armagh and parts of Co Londonderry, and ceded a chunk of Donegal. But the Boundary Commission's recommendations were leaked and, following an outcry from some politicians in the Irish Free State and some Ulster Unionists, were shelved. Had they been implemented, much subsequent anguish might have been averted: South Armagh, the terrorist epicentre during the Troubles, would have been part of the Irish Republic.

In India, the failure was even greater. The boundary line was imposed more or less arbitrarily by Mountbatten. The demand of the Muslim League for separate statehood was neither granted nor denied, but – the worst option of all – half-implemented. More Muslims were left in India than in Pakistan, and parts of the border bore no relation whatever to local preferences. These regions – above all, Kashmir, whose promised plebiscite was never held – have been in a state of semi-permanent conflict ever since, serving to poison relations between Pakistan and India.

In any case, it is misleading to hold up the worst cases as typical. There are plenty of examples of peaceful divorces, from Czechoslovakia to the West Indies Federation. It's true that the interspersing of populations can be a complicating factor. Yugoslavia is often cited as a textbook example of why partition is wrong, and the EU's determination to maintain the territorial integrity of Bosnia-Herzegovina is sometimes justified as an attempt to prevent a repeat of the horrors of the early 1990s. In fact, the way to have avoided those horrors would have been through a series of plebiscites, overseen by neutral observers. The resulting borders would have been almost exactly what they are now – with the difference that it might not have been necessary to fight a monstrous series of wars to secure them.

Had the international community accepted the case for national self-determination at the outset, and offered to mediate a series of votes and, where necessary, voluntary population exchanges, we might have been spared the horrors of war and ethnic cleansing. Instead, when Slovenia, in a referendum held on 23 December 1990, became the first state to declare independence, following a referendum in which 94.8 per cent of those taking part (and an extraordinary 88.5 per cent of all eligible voters) opted for secession, the EU responded by insisting on the territorial integrity of Yugoslavia. It announced that any states which withdrew from the federation would be denied trade and aid accords. Only when the war had destroyed the old state did it reluctantly recognise the reality of Croatian and Slovenian independence.

The EU's distrust of the nation state is perhaps most obvious in its relations with Israel. No state in the world so clearly embodies the national principle. For 2,000 years, Jews were scattered and stateless, but never lost their aspiration to statehood: 'Next year in Jerusalem'. If Israel's claim is valid – if people are truly better off living in their own national groups – then everything the EU has done since its foundation in 1957 is questionable. Which is why, in recent years, Brussels has shifted from a more-or-less uncomplicatedly pro-Palestinian position (the EU has long been the chief financial sponsor of the Palestinian entity in its various forms) to calling for regional integration and a dismantling of barriers. Israelis sometimes blame this attitude on anti-Americanism, or anti-Semitism. In fact, the EU is being perfectly consistent, rejecting national claims abroad as it does within its own territory.

Democracy is not simply a periodic right to mark a cross on a ballot paper. It also depends upon a relationship between government and governed, on a sense of common affinity and allegiance. To put it another way, democracy requires a *demos*: a unit with which we identify when we use the word 'we'. Take away the *demos* and you are left only with the *kratos*: with the power of a state that must compel by force of law what it cannot ask in the name of civic patriotism. In the absence of a *demos*, governments are even likelier than usual to purchase votes through, for example, public works schemes and sinecures. One way to think about the EU is as a massive vehicle for the redistribution of wealth. Taxpayers in all the states contribute (though their contributions are hidden among the national tax-takes), and the revenue is then used to buy the loyalty of articulate and powerful groups: consultants, contractors, big landowners, NGOs, corporations, charities and municipalities.

To many Euro-integrationists, political assimilation is a greater goal than democracy or the rule of law. When countries vote 'No' to closer union, their verdict is swatted aside in defiance both of the democratic principle and of the EU's own rules. Indeed, the President of the European Commission, José Manuel Durão Barroso, argued in 2010 that nation states were dangerous precisely because they were excessively democratic: 'Governments are not always right. If governments were always right we would not have the situation that we have today. Decisions taken by the most democratic institutions in the world are very often wrong.' This is, of course, a reaffirmation of de Gaulle's remark about democracy and national sovereignty being the same thing, the only difference being that Mr Barroso sees both concepts as undesirable.

In our reflection on the right of national self-determination, it is worth touching on the case against international jurisdiction more widely. The past twenty years have witnessed a revolution. It has been carried out quietly and bloodlessly, but it is, in its way, as far-reaching a revolution as those of 1789 or 1917. The rule that had governed relations between states since the Treaty of Westphalia of 1648 – the principle that each government was responsible for its internal affairs, and that crimes were the responsibility of the state on whose territory they were committed – has been overturned. A new legal order has been established, outside and above the nations. The new order does not take its authority from a single treaty or charter. It is protean, residing in the hundreds of international accords, conventions and declarations that national courts treat as precedent. Nor is it limited in scope. Far from restricting itself to international questions, it presumes to regulate all manner of internal matters: the rights of refugees, the status of children, employment law, religious freedom and so on. A corpus of law has been created without discussion, without debate by national legislatures, without democratic approval. Its motive force has been the activism of judges and the intimidating fervour of human rights professionals in various UN-sponsored institutions, lobby groups and, not least, the private legal practices that have grown up over the past twenty years to exploit the new jurisprudence. So far, proponents of international governance have had it almost all their own way. In plush conference venues around the world, out from under the public eye, they have enlarged and developed their jurisdiction. Funded by the global NGOs and by UN agencies, they have had time and resources, motive and opportunity. Hardly anyone, by contrast, seems to have much incentive to speak up for the majority.

Territorial jurisdiction has been a remarkably successful concept. Ever since the Treaty of Westphalia, it has been broadly understood that crimes are the responsibility of the state where they are committed. Untune that string, and hark, what discord follows! Western liberals might say: 'Since Radovan Karadzic won't get justice in Serbia, he should get it at The Hague.' But an Iranian judge might apply precisely the same logic and say: 'Adulterers in Western countries are going unpunished: we must kidnap them and bring them to a place where they will face consequences.' International jurisdiction breaks the link between legislators and law. Instead of legislation being passed by representatives who are, in some way, accountable to their populations, laws are generated by international jurists. We are, in other words, reverting to the pre-modern notion that law-givers should be accountable to their own consciences rather than to those who must live under their rulings.

In consequence, as Robert Bork has argued in *Coercing Virtue: The Worldwide Rule of Judges*, an agenda is being advanced which has been rejected at the ballot box. Courts make tendentious and expansive interpretations of human rights codes, which go well beyond what any reasonable person would take the text to mean. With no meaningful scrutiny, international lawyers, prosecutors and judges are able to suit themselves, meandering their way through gargantuan budgets, changing their own rules when they become inconvenient. As John Laughland showed in his study of the Milosevic trial, the UN International Criminal Tribunal for the former Yugoslavia admitted hearsay evidence, repeatedly amended its rules of procedure and, when the old brute proved surprisingly eloquent in his own defence, took the extraordinary step of imposing counsel on him. Eight years and $200 million later, with the court no closer to a verdict, both judge and defendant were dead. These objections lose none of their force simply because Slobodan Milosevic was a bad man. Bad men – bad men especially, one could argue – deserve justice. Indicting a head of state – as the ICC did in 2009 when it served a writ against the Sudanese President – amounts to declaring a war which one has no intention of fighting. The only way to bring President Bashir to trial would be to conquer his country and transfer sovereignty from him to the occupying powers: the basis of the Allies' jurisdiction at the Nuremberg trials. Without such a determination, international arraignments are declamatory: a way for those who serve them to feel good about themselves, even though their practical effect is to make tyrants dig in more deeply.

While tyrants ignore international rulings, democracies – or, more precisely, judges *within* democracies – don't. Courts in Western countries increasingly use international conventions to challenge the decisions of their elected governments. Four successive Labour Home Secretaries have tried unsuccessfully to repatriate the Afghan hijackers who diverted a flight at gunpoint to Stansted. Despite the nature of their crime, and despite the removal of the Taliban regime from which they claimed to be fleeing, they have been granted leave to remain in the United Kingdom through, in effect, judicial activism.

Let me return, in closing, to Charles de Gaulle's observation that national sovereignty and democracy are the same thing. It is not enough for a country to hold elections within an agreed unit. The results of those elections must be meaningful. The representatives chosen at them should be the lawmakers. We are in danger of setting aside a trusted and workable system of international relations almost whimsically; certainly without a meaningful debate. It is time that debate took place. Against this onslaught of international jurisdiction – blocking the emergence of nationhood abroad and eroding democracy at home – the right to secede takes on a whole new, provocative meaning.

Part III
Losing and Finding Our History

Chris Husbands

– 5: Nations and Their Pasts –

When did the Second World War start?[1] There is a standard, very quick answer to this typical assessment question: the Second World War began in September 1939 when Germany invaded Poland and when Britain and France declared war on Germany. But it turns out that this is only a partial answer. It is plausible enough to argue that the Second World War really began in July 1937, when the Second Sino-Japanese war broke out following the Marco Polo Bridge incident and the Japanese assault on Beijing, which turned the intermittent skirmishes of the previous six years into full blown war. A case can be made for the Second World War beginning in 1940, when military activity began in western Europe with the German invasion of the Low Countries and France, bringing British troops into active combat for the first time, extensively, since the declaration of war in September 1939. A very strong contender is the year 1941, which first saw the Nazi invasion of the Soviet Union in June and then the American entry into the war following the Japanese attack on Pearl Harbor in December. Lastly, it could be reasoned that World War II truly began in 1919 with the signing of the Treaty of Versailles. Five possible candidates: 1919, 1937, 1939, 1940, 1941 – which one to pick?

Like Toynbee, we have to resist 'the dogma that History is just "one damned thing after another"':[2] understanding the past involves managing complex information and deploying it around some difficult underlying questions. While a historical question might appear deceptively simple, it entails several challenges. The first is that answering it involves the deployment of a range, albeit a general one, of historical knowledge, itself based on the ability to sequence information and to put the sequence into an analytical order. The second is that answering it makes the respondent reflect carefully on assumptions: those of us schooled in England will normally reach, almost unthinkingly for the answer '1939'. This, after all is how the conflict is memorialised on war memorials throughout the country. But this might be an answer to the question 'When did Britain declare war on Germany?' rather than the set question with which this essay began. A third aspect of the question lies in its challenge to world views, prompting a careful reflection on what is meant by the 'Second World War', as well as by a war 'starting'.

Well-chosen questions in history shift perceptions about the past at the same time as they involve the acquisition of historical knowledge; they pose sharp intellectual puzzles. *What happened in India in 1857?*: lazily, we might argue that the answer is the Indian Mutiny, but of course Indians at the time – and since –

did not describe it as such. For nationalists, 1857 was presented as the first blow in the struggle to free India from imperial rule.[3] The different sort of language, the different sorts of ideas which are coded into the language, rapidly open up the questions about what the events meant and the meanings which were subsequently given to them. *Why was the Dutch invasion of England in 1688 so quickly presented as being un-Dutch? Why was the German victory at Waterloo seized as a British triumph, secured on the 'playing fields of Eton'?* These are mildly subversive questions, which begin to unpick a sense of the national past, which is so often taken for granted. All of these interrogations problematise history in challenging ways, teasing away at the relationship between what we know, our relationship with the past and the nature of the 'stories' we share or might disagree about. Those are the very themes we grapple with when thinking about the history and the nature of the nation.

But before going any further, we have to ask ourselves the really very difficult, yet fundamental question about what 'history' actually is. The word itself shelters several etymological roots and ideas. Herodotus, writing in the early fifth century BCE, used the term 'historia' (στορία), which was literally an 'enquiry'.[4] Herodotus had a specific question for his enquiry: why was the Persian Empire unable to conquer the Greek city states? The principle of constructing an account of the past in response to a specific question is as old as the concept of 'history' itself. For Herodotus the failure of the Persian assault on the Greek cities was explained culturally and socially: the forces of Persian slavery were defeated by Athenian freedom and Greek unity. He was writing about the past in terms of his own present: ironically at the time that Herodotus was writing, Athens had become imperialist itself. Alongside στορία there are other ideas in the word 'history'. The French term *l'histoire* translates as both history and story, the narrative threads of actions, consequences and reactions. John Burrow traced the development of history from Herodotus through early Christian scholars to sixteenth century humanists and on to those nineteenth century historians who had enormous confidence about the possibility of producing a definitive account of human experience. He identified common themes: the relationship between enquiry and story, the remoteness and oddness of the past and radically different ideas about the relationship between the past and the present. Sometimes historians' ideas are of decline and loss, sometimes of steady if uneven progress, sometimes of a working out of destiny, whether Christian, liberal or Marxist. Burrow concludes that 'almost all historians except the very dullest have some characteristic weakness: some complicity, idealisation, identification; some impulse to indignation, to right wrongs, *to deliver a message*. It is often the source of their most interesting writing.'⁵ What we call history rests on our relationship with the past.

If this is true of what historians do, it is no less true of history in schools: the school history curriculum and the individual lessons that make up pupils' experiences are driven by choices about content, what purposes content serves, and ideas we have about our relationships with it. Canadian academics such as Peter Seixas have written extensively about the importance of 'historical consciousness', which they described as 'individual and collective understandings of the past, the cognitive and cultural factors which shape those understandings, as well as the relations of historical understandings to those of the present and the future.'[6]

More recently, and more contentiously, the idea of a 'usable past' has been developed to denote an understanding of the past that people can use to help orientate themselves in time, rather than the more commonly used term of 'utility' which implies a past that serves functions ascribed by others, such as being a good citizen.[7] Marx and Engels wrote the *Communist Manifesto* in just this way, to show fighters on the barricades in 1848 exactly where, in Marx and Engels view, they stood in the dialectical struggle of class warfare, and therefore, what they were fighting for and what the result of their actions might be. Similarly, national liberation movements in former colonies placed a premium upon finding the earliest plausible examples of resistance as a way of bolstering their present status or in some cases of creating the myth of a history that they would have liked to have had, but which did not actually occur.

What is in common here – and is implied in both the ready answer about the opening of the Second World War and the more complex variants – is the idea that the learning of history involves the acquisition of ideas about the past, shaping understanding of the present as much as of the past, and shuttling between everyday and 'academic' understandings of a shared past.

This idea is not new. A shared identity seeks to define the nation. In Britain, Linda Colley has argued, the idea of a nation was created in the eighteenth century:[8] to be British was defined against an external 'other', to be anti-Catholic and anti-French. Colley emphasised the important role which almost continual warfare with France played in the 'forging' and defining of a British national identity, which united Scots, Welsh and English. Britishness existed alongside, and not in competition with, attachment to England, Wales and Scotland. Colley tracked the ways in which Britain and the British were historically created by the integration of the constituent regions of England, Wales and Scotland, and the idea of a shared national present and past were thereby shaped.

History as an academic discipline found its way into English universities in the nineteenth century at about the same time as compulsory elementary education was developed, with history as a part of the common curriculum. Interest in the national past across Europe in the mid-nineteenth century has been described as being part of the process of creation of a shared national past at a time when the modern nation state was being forged with all its accompaniments: national uniforms, national dress, national anthems, national school systems. For nineteenth century nationalists, the study of national history in developing civic universities and in developing elementary school systems was of a piece: the nation was being shaped through the codification of histories of the past and for marshalling the present and – in the libraries, archives and classrooms, the future. Milan Kundera, writing in a quite different context, captured it perfectly: 'People are always shouting they want to create a better future. It's not true. The future is an apathetic void of no interest to anyone. The past is full of life, eager to irritate us, provoke and insult us, tempt us to destroy or repaint it. The only reason people want to be masters of the future is to change the past.'[9] And politicians since the nineteenth century have seen history as an important political and ideological battleground. As Marc Ferro carefully documented, history was shaped and twisted for use by governments of all ideological suasions throughout the twentieth century: Germanic history for the schools of Nazi Germany, racist history for the schools of apartheid South Africa, socialist history for the schools of Soviet Russia.[10] Mikhail Gorbachev famously cancelled national high school history examinations in the USSR in the late 1980s because, he said, there was no point in testing pupils' knowledge of lies.[11]

History teaching in England's schools has always been closely tied up with the idea of the nation, though the idea coalesced in the later nineteenth century. Valerie Chancellor traced the development of what she called, in her 1970 account, 'history for their masters'.[12] History texts, traced by Chancellor from the middle of the 1850s typically offered a catechism of history, with questions and brief answers. The texts were dull: the Taunton Report of 1868 pointed out that 'neither knowledge nor interest is excited by the sort of manuals it is now profitable to work at.'[13] In the later nineteenth century, history texts became more jingoistic as the curriculum coalesced around an idea of the English past entirely recognisable from Colley's account; figures such as Drake, Grenville, Marlborough, Wolfe, Clive, Nelson and Wellington, as well as the Victorian favourites, Havelock and Gordon, came to predominate, with a marked tendency to focus on the triumphs of a shared Protestant past and wars with France – clearly echoing the concept of Britishness which emerged in Colley's account of the later eighteenth century. Textbooks celebrated the English constitutional settlement, and were clearly against revolutionary doctrine, and even against the Chartists.[14] The texts were designed to educate the rising generation to uphold the traditions of society, rather than to reform them. Clear opinions were expressed about morality and the virtue of thrift; most writers had exalted views of Britain's achievement and place in the world. While the monarchy was sacrosanct, individual kings were often subjected to fierce scrutiny.

This version of a shared, 'British' national past was hugely influential throughout the twentieth century, shaping what David Sylvester memorably called 'the great tradition' of history teaching. In the 'great tradition' the history teacher's role was 'didactically active; it was to give pupils the facts of historical knowledge and to ensure through repeated short tests that they had learned them. The pupil's role was passive; history was a "received subject". The body of knowledge to be taught was also clearly defined. It was mainly political history, with some European, from Julius Caesar to 1914.'[15] In somewhat different terms, John Slater teased readers about the underlying assumptions of the knowledge base of this great tradition 'content was largely British, or rather Southern English; Celts looked in to starve, emigrate, or rebel; the North to invent looms or work in mills; abroad was of interest once it was part of the Empire; foreigners were either, sensibly, allies, or, rightly, defeated'.[16] Richard Evans teases his readers still further: this was the history of the 'wonderfulness of us'.[17]

Of course, the nation of the early twenty-first century is different from the nation of the later nineteenth century, both in its make up and its version of itself. More demographically and culturally diverse, with quite different views of, for example, the histories and rights of women and of minority groups. The experience of war, which shaped the history curriculum of the later nineteenth century, has not survived accounts of total war of the twentieth century. The history curriculum has changed markedly over the course of the later twentieth century. Sylvester's 'great tradition' broke down increasingly from the later 1960s under a series of powerful challenges, though the breakdown was partial, ragged and more complex than some popular accounts of the impact of what was at the time called the 'new history'. The transformation of academic history, with increased focus on social and economic histories – often uncovering the uncomfortable complexities of historical change and giving, in E. P. Thompson's striking phrase a 'voice to the voiceless'[18] – played a significant role, as new history teachers entered the profession with more diverse insights than their predecessors. The transformation of urban school populations in the wake of large scale migration provided another basis for re-appraisal of the content of the school curriculum. What evidence there is suggests that in practice, the school curricula of the 1970s and 1980s, however, remained doggedly whiggish: the abolition of the slave trade, the amelioration of factory conditions in the nineteenth century, the rise of modern public health and medical science, and the progressive emancipation of women were central themes of most history syllabi.[19] This powerful overarching narrative tended, through most of the period to crowd out some of the more awkward content areas. Thus, for example, the abolition of the slave trade provided a comforting account of humanitarian triumph rather than an opportunity to confront the extent to which English merchant fortunes were grounded on the proceeds of human trafficking. In this respect, English history curricula were quite different from what we know of contemporary American curricula. The Second World War provided an opportunity to celebrate national self-sacrifice and triumph over adversity, with little widespread attention to the Holocaust: only in the 1990s was the Holocaust regarded as a compulsory element of the secondary curriculum. In this respect, English history curricula were quite similar to American curricula.[20]

Throughout the 1970s, 1980s and 1990s, the relationship between the history curriculum and the idea of the nation became increasingly complex as both shifted: the one through shifting ideas about history as a discipline – less *l'histoire* and more στορία – the other as demographic, social and political change disrupted many of the certainties had underpinned the idea of the nation in classrooms in the later nineteenth and early twentieth centuries. The 1980s in particular were a period of ferocious debate about the curriculum. The introduction of a national curriculum by Mrs Thatcher's government in 1988 – the first time that a national curriculum had been prescribed in England since 1903 – brought the debates into the open. There were – of course – strident voices urging different perspectives; for many cultural conservatives the national curriculum provided above all an opportunity to reinforce the 'great tradition'. The then Secretary of State, Kenneth Baker, sent a direct instruction to the chair of the History Working Group that the 'programmes of study should have at their core the history of Britain, the record of its past and in particular its political, constitutional and cultural heritage'.[21] Conversely, cultural radicals emphasised the need for explorations of different traditions.[22] The recommendations of the History Working Group in many ways eschewed both extremes through the device of requiring an assessment of pupils' understandings of 'interpretations of history'. That way, it was emphasised that the relationship between the history curriculum and the idea of the nation depended both on the way the past was viewed and the way the present was understood.[23] Because after all nations, no less than ideas about history, shift and change.

The debate on 'Britishness' has accelerated during the first decade of the twenty-first century for a variety of reasons ranging from devolution and evolution of the European Union to the rise of the BNP[24] and acts of terrorism carried out by British citizens. In a conference about Britishness convened by the Fabian Society in 2006, Gordon Brown, then Labour Chancellor, referred to the need to wrest the Union Jack away from the BNP and to use it as a 'symbol of unity' emphasising values of fairness, liberty and responsibility 'which run like a 'golden thread' through Britain's past'.[25] David Cameron subsequently used a speech at the Greatest Briton of 2005 award ceremony to outline his own views on the subject, claiming that Britishness is not about flags, but rather that 'reserve is an intrinsic part of being British'. Both saw a key role for history lessons in shaping the sense of a collective identity. Even the singer Billy Bragg, long associated with the radical left, warned at the Fabian conference that 'if we flinch from a discussion of our history, we leave it to the BNP and UKIP[26] – it's a nettle we must grasp.'

The issues at stake are complex, not least because there is no consensus around the values associated with being British. In contrast to Brown and Cameron above, the newspaper columnist Yasmin Alibhai-Brown, herself a refugee created by Idi Amin's expulsion of Asians from Uganda, regards the concept of universally good British values as 'absurd' and sees the challenge as the creation of 'a new British identity which has evolved from historical meanings but is not bound by history'.[27] In other words, Britishness is an identity which reflects the realities of the present rather than being dependent on past actions and values. In Linda Colley's words, it expresses 'an invented nation superimposed . . . onto much older alignments and loyalties'.[28] Increasingly the argument is made that the cultural diversity of the population itself requires an emphasis on the lineages of political, economic and cultural history *within* these islands: in other words, that the nation needs 'reinventing' for the twenty-first century.

If this is true, it surely follows that the 'island story' of the later nineteenth and early twentieth centuries alone will not, in itself, be fit for purpose. History has changed: the nineteenth century account of a national story with England at the core has been replaced in historiography by histories of the 'Isles',[29] and the social histories of voices 'hidden from history' have crowded in. The nation's sense of its position has changed, its relationships with Empire and Europe have been reconfigured – albeit, in the case of the latter, plainly still unresolved. And the nation has changed: more intricate, more multicultural, with ethnic, cultural and sexual identities all acknowledged as more complex. The tensions between identity and relativism, between the nation and the individual are real. Many teachers are suspicious of using history to promote a sense of British identity precisely because of the obvious abuses of the subject in the school curriculum of the later nineteenth century. As one respondent to Alison Kitson's study of the teaching of history in post-conflict situations said, he would 'hate to be teaching a subject which is about Britain's greatness . . . there are lots of things we should be proud of but also things we shouldn't.'[30] Nevertheless, teachers have been teaching mainly British – indeed, English – history at key stage 3 for much of the twentieth century and when pushed to identify those topics which all pupils should learn about, most respondents in my own study of the aims of history teaching cited events and people drawn from Britain's past.[31] There seems to be consensus that pupils ought to learn about British history, but there is room for considerable debate about how much of their history curriculum should be made up of British history and about the way this history is presented, and nuanced. Teachers need to be outward as well as inward looking in the ways they teach Britain's past. One of the defining features of Britain lies in its relationship to the rest of the world, from its earliest origins in the waves of invasion and settlement to the expansion of the Empire and its collapse.

Identity, diversity and nationhood are challenging ideas. Keith Ajegbo, who led a review of citizenship and diversity for Government in 2005, argued that history is a component of citizenship education because of its role in exploring identity and diversity in the UK. History, Ajegbo argued, can bring 'rigour to the debate'[32] whilst retaining its integrity as an academic component of the curriculum. In Northern Ireland, where the historical roots of conflicting identities are especially resonant, teachers have traditionally shied away from tackling issues of identity, or indeed anything controversial, overtly. The most recent research suggests that consequently, pupils take what they want from the past to justify their preconceptions, whether that be from history classrooms or from elsewhere.[33] But there is compelling evidence that history can help pupils to explore challenging issues of conflict and identity, whereas when history teachers avoid tackling controversial issues pupils are likely to draw on 'street' knowledge which reinforces conventional misunderstandings. At the same time, if history is to play a part in education for diversity and interdependence, much of the traditional content of school history needs revision: the past, in schools, needs to be fit for the present. We teach history as part of a curriculum which seeks to prepare young people for adult life. The experiences of the Isles and the people who have lived here provide a window on the history of the world, but a history curriculum which is not open to the world is unlikely to prepare young people for understanding a world of global interdependence. The balance between local, national and global, between different perspectives needs open exploration – once again, back to those disturbing, perspective-shifting questions.

Notes

1 I am grateful to my colleague Dylan Wiliam for the suggested question. The way it is used here is my own.
2 Toynbee, A., *A Study of History, Abridgement of Volumes VII-X* (1987; Oxford: Oxford University Press), p.267.
3 cf. S. Sen, 'Eighteen Fifty Seven' in Stokes, E., *The Peasant and the Raj: Studies in agrarian cociety and peasant rebellion in colonial India* (1980; Cambridge: Cambridge University Press).
4 Burrow, J., *A History of Histories: Epics, Chronicles, Romances and Inquiries from Herodotus and Thucydides to the Twentieth Century* (2009; London: Allen Lane).
5 Ibid., p.51, emphasis added.

6 Laville, C., 'Historical Consciousness and the Historical
   Education: What to Expect from the First to the Second', in
   P. Seixas, *Theorising Historical Consciousness* (2006; Toronto:
   University of Toronto Press). Seixas, P., 'Historical Understanding among Adolescents in a Multicultural Setting',
   Curriculum Inquiry (1993), 23(3). Seixas, P., 'A discipline
   adrift in an integrated curriculum: history in British Columbia schools', *Canadian Journal of Education* (1994), 19(1):
   99–107; and http://www.cshc.ubc.ca/about.php.
7 Howson, J., 2009. 'Potential and pitfalls in teaching "big
   pictures" of the past', *Teaching History* (2009), 136: 24–33.
8 Colley, L., *Britons: Forging the Nation* (1992; Yale: Yale
   University Press).
9 Kundera, M., *The Book of Laughter and Forgetting* (1980;
   New York: Knopf), p.22.
10 Ferro, M., *The Use and Abuse of History: or, How the past is
   taught to children* (1984; London: Routledge & Kegan Paul).
11 Esther B. Fein, 'Moscow Summit: Unmaking History and
   Debating Rights; Soviet Pupils Spared Exams While History
   is Rewritten', *New York Times*, 31 May 1988.
12 Chancellor, V., *History for Their Masters: Opinion in the
   English History Textbook, 1800–1914* (1970; Bath: Adams
   and Dart).
13 The reference to Taunton is from D. Beales, *The Student's
   Text Book of English and General History* (1901; London).
14 Chartism was the first mass working class labour movement
   in the world in the first half of the nineteenth century.
15 Sylvester, D., 'Change and continuity in history teaching
   1900–93', in Bourdillon, H., (ed.), *Teaching History: A Reader*
   (1994; London: Routledge in association with The Open
   University).
16 Slater, J., *The Politics of History Teaching: A Humanity
   Dehumanized?* (1989; London: Institute of Education), p.1.
17 Evans, R., 'The Wonderfulness of Us', *London Review of
   Books*, 17 March 2011.
18 Thompson, E. P., *The Making of the English Working Class*
   (1965; Harmondsworth: Penguin).

19 Cannadine, D., *The Right Kind of History* (2012; London: Palgrave).

20 Fallace, T. D., *The Emergence of Holocaust Education in American Schools* (2008; New York: Palgrave Macmillan).

21 Quoted in Phillips, R., *History Teaching, Nationhood and the State: a study in educational politics* (1998; London: Cassell), p.57.

22 Pankhania, J., *Liberating the History National Curriculum* (1994; Lewes: Falmer Press); Sherwood, M., 'SOS: Is Anybody Listening?', *Teaching History*, June 1994.

23 Phillips, op. cit., pp. 62–4.

24 British National Party, a far-right political party.

25 Brown, G., *Keynote Speech: The Future of Britishness* (2006; Fabian Society Conference).

26 UK Independence Party, a right-wing Eurosceptic party.

27 Alibhai-Brown, Y., 'Who are we and what do we want to be?', *Guardian*, 2006: http://www.guardian.co.uk/politics/2006/jan/13/thinktanks.uk.

28 Colley, op. cit., p.4.

29 See, for an example, Kearney, H., *The British Isles: A History of Four Nations* (1989; Cambridge: Cambridge University Press).

30 Kitson, A., 'History Teaching and Reconciliation in Northern Ireland', in E. A. Cole (ed.), *Teaching the Violent Past* (2005; Lanham, Maryland, Rowman and Littlefield).

31 Husbands, C., Kitson, A. and Pendry, A., *Understanding History Teaching. Teaching and learning about the past in secondary schools* (2003; Maidenhead: Open University Press/McGraw-Hill Education).

32 Ajegbo, K., *Curriculum Review: Diversity and Citizenship* (2007; Report Number: 00045-2007, DOM-EN London, Department for Education and Skills).

33 McCully, A., and N. Pilgrim, N., '"They took Ireland away from us and we've got to fight to get it back." Using fictional characters to explore the relationship between historical interpretation and contemporary attitudes', *Teaching History* (2007) 114: 17–22.

Frank Field

– 6: Power on the Move:
England, Whose England? –

England in a double bind

E ngland finds herself in a double bind. The first bind is what the editors, in their Introduction, term the 'ascendant narrative', which views the nation state as 'pathological in its very nature'. According to this view nation states, which have so often been the cause of war, must have their teeth, in the form of sovereignty, drawn out to prevent conflict arising. In Europe, for example, in order to prevent war again engulfing Europe and beyond, we have put in place supra-national institutions, most obviously the European Union (EU). This has eroded democracy in the EU member states through the transfer of more and more power to Brussels.

This erosion of democracy is well enough understood – although more clearly by the British electorate than by the Westminster political class, or indeed by the media where most editorial opinion does not reflect the balance of opinion in the country.

By and large, across the centre-left to the centre-right spectrum, British elected representatives are caught between a rock and a hard place. They are trapped between growing popular resentment of the EU and a resigned sense of the difficulty of undoing the many threads that tie the country into EU institutions and processes. Of course some idealists (mostly in minority parties) still believe in the EU dream of emulating America's 'ever closer union', which most recently led to the creation of the euro. The single currency is however currently and dangerously chewing up democracy in fragile parts of the Continent only recently freed from dictatorships. The truth is that most British politicians take the line of least resistance: now we are in, we had better make the best job of it – although there is seemingly precious little determination to work for reform from the inside. The unspoken truth is that a lot of British politicians could be forgiven for envying former colleagues who having failed in domestic politics, made it big and rich in Brussels. They ogle the EU gravy-train that is free from the annoyance of electors, who merely foot the bill.

The second bind is, as we will see, entwined with the first although it arises from a different source. The second bind is the long-term refusal of Britain's political class to recognise, as they wind down the UK's status in the world, the legitimate aspirations of England as the dominant partner of the old Union – the United Kingdom.

Following the break-up of the British Empire, the largest territorial interest ever built, Scotland, Wales and Northern Ireland began to adjust to these strange circumstances, perhaps opportunistically, by successfully asserting an identity that had been submerged in a UK-led operation. The assertion of nationhood by three of the four constituent parts of the UK has however left England exposed, and the leadership of all three main political parties has prevented England from following the same path as the other countries of the UK, despite England's dominance in the UK Ltd enterprise. Size and wealth cannot continue to be a (perhaps unexpected) barrier to a legitimate expression of England's nationhood.

Devolution has helped to maintain a sense of legitimacy for politics in many parts of the UK. But instead of making England central to the debate, England's importance, and even her name, have been systematically airbrushed out of any conversation about constitutional reform. To add insult to injury, England has even been denied the right to assert her separate identity from the other nations of the United Kingdom. This state of affairs, in its most insidious form, is mirrored by the insistence on calling British all that is English.[1] And it is full of danger.

As a country England is in new constitutional waters. Up until now, as power moved from one institution to another, Britain's ancient but largely unwritten constitution had adapted itself remarkably well. Major shifts in power had been able to take place almost effortlessly and without any rupture of the political fabric and governing institutions of the country.[2] Since the Act of Union with Scotland in 1707, a national history stressing Britain over its component parts has provided the necessary putty to keep a unitary state together.

Devolution has abruptly ruptured the workings of that constitution. It has also laid bare the contradictions of our recent national narrative, which confuses Britain and England, often to the detriment of the latter. Years ago the witty raconteur Michael Flanders observed that whenever something good happened, then it was 'a triumph for Great Britain' and whenever the opposite occurred, 'England loses again'! This should not continue. Perhaps it was unintentional in the minds of those who have promoted devolution – although they may have had narrower motives of factional self-interest in mind – but England has been awoken in the process. Devolution must begin to meet the legitimate demands of the English to assert their identity. England is resurfacing.

I do not pretend that this is easy for today's Labour Party, for both historical and more immediate reasons. But the Labour Party must engage with the trend. It has to understand the consequences of being held culpable by much of the electorate for England's continued suppression during the New Labour years.

History shows that Labour only wins well when it is able to reach beyond its core vote and here is part of its electoral challenge. As Jimmy Thomas, the inter-war railway man turned cabinet minister often remarked, if one could not ride two horses at once then one should not be part of the political circus. Part of the appeal, both to Labour's core vote and to the public as a whole, must be made by striking a proper patriotic note.

That would be the blunt message to his successors from Ernest Bevin, Foreign Secretary in Labour's most successful administration, Clement Attlee's great post-war Labour Government. Tony Blair learned this lesson early from his defeat in the Beaconsfield by-election which took place during the Falklands War. It was a lesson he never forgot, and whatever people think of 'Blair's Wars', he alone of all Labour leaders has matched Mrs Thatcher's achievement of winning three general elections outright. I think however that Labour needs to disentangle this electoral lesson from the actions of the Blair and Brown years. It needs to express naturally the love of one's country with which so much of the electorate wishes to be associated. Helping Labour do just this has always been part of my mission in politics.

The air is full of irony at this point. Labour has an outstanding record in leading the country, from the days of Empire to the establishment of the Commonwealth. Yet the crude deprecation of all things associated with the Empire has overwhelmed the Party's confidence in setting this record within its proper historical context. The prevailing narrative takes no notice of the more nuanced picture now painted by modern historians, and the much more balanced view of the British Empire that is emerging, much of it coming from historians in Commonwealth countries.

According to the seminal work of socialist theorist Benedict Anderson,[3] communities are more fundamentally things for the mind than of the physical world. If our 'imagined communities' cease to excite us, then they die. That insight shaped the historian Linda Colley's influential account of how the British identity came to excite the vast majority of people between the Act of Union in 1707 and Queen Victoria's accession in 1837. As Chris Husbands also discusses in this volume, Colley's main explanation was that the identity of 'Britons' was forged in adversity to the French in the succession of wars in which, directly or indirectly, the Hanoverian crown was pitched against a common enemy. For this period therefore, Britishness was not an English imposition on resentful Celts. It could and did exist alongside older identities. Great Britain was 'an invented nation superimposed, if only for a while, onto much older alignments and loyalties'.[4] We Britons felt our togetherness in contrast to the 'otherness' of our enemies, and that meant the French. Scots and Welsh filled the ranks of the armies that fought those wars and that latterly policed the Empire.

That British identity was maintained and affirmed by the role the constituent parts of the UK had in building and maintaining the Empire. Yet for England, and in particular for Labour, 'Britishness' retained the taint of Empire long after the Empire had disappeared. Other parts of the UK have in large part lessened the political anguish associated with the loss of Empire and world power status by reasserting their own national identity. The political elite at the national level, however, strongly Scottish on the Labour side, has prevented England from doing the same.

Thus a major country, as England is in terms of size, population and wealth, is being denied any role in determining its own future – at a time when the British constitution no longer acts as the framework for what was once a unitary state. England finds herself part of an incoherent association of countries with varying powers, which all hold different relationships with the former governing centre at Westminster. One distinguishing mark in this incoherence is that England, and only England, does not have an assembly or Parliament for debate and decision making on exclusively English matters.

The peculiarity of the English

The refusal to admit England as active participant in this process of striking constitutional change prevents the English constitution from evolving incrementally to reflect new patterns of power and influence, as it has done so often in the past. This is both new and disturbing in these islands. But it is not unfamiliar in Europe. Since the time of the Treaty of Westphalia, when constitution-making began to contest the concept of divine right, continental European states have typically experienced trauma as regimes have changed, because constitutions could only be reshaped after first being broken.

Edmund Burke, after observing events in France in 1789 published within an astonishingly short time his reflections on the French Revolution.[5] Burke illuminated here some of those key features of England that have made this nation systematically different from the continent and, in my view, a safer place. Burke sketched aspects of that essential inclusiveness which has lain on top of a pattern of land ownership coupled to obligation, mediated through the common law, which has existed for far longer than any differently formulated patterns of rights and obligations to be found in Europe.[6]

Recent studies of the English Civil War illustrate just how different the roles and relationships of the Crown, aristocracy and gentry were from the Continental experience of revolution. It may be awkward for Marxist historians, but the fact is that many of the great aristocratic families (Lord Burghley's family, the Cecils, for example, who descended from Elizabeth I's Chancellor) were much sooner enemies of Charles I and active in removing absolute monarchy than was once thought.[7] Similarly, it was the heroic aristocrat Lord Russell, the Whig leader who was executed in 1683 on trumped-up charges of treason by Charles

II (and then posthumously pardoned by William of Orange (William III) after the Glorious Revolution of 1688) who is rightly acclaimed as a founder of the constitutional settlement which has permitted representative democracy under a constitutional monarchy to flourish in the UK.

All this may be thought to be awkward for a man of the Left to admit. But I find no more difficulty than did George Orwell, who explained more passionately and succinctly than anyone how English patriotism and a zeal for social change can combine. It is not without significance that Orwell subtitled his major work on this theme Socialism and the English Genius. Patriotism was as natural to Orwell as breathing. This did not prevent him for a moment from being highly critical of those aspects of the Empire of which he had had first-hand experience and of which he disapproved. But neither did it stop him from appreciating what is now seen as the positive side of what Britain did beyond its borders. Orwell, for example, fought against fascism in Spain and in the Second World War. Nor did his wish for a more equal society prevent him from knowing what was achievable. In one passage of his essay *The Lion and the Unicorn* Orwell states the case for limitations of income 'so that the highest tax free income in Britain does not exceed the lowest by more than 10-1'.[8] Two pages later he adds: 'in practice it is impossible that earnings should be limited quite as rigidly'.[9]

There are good reasons why English socialism

developed the cultural qualities of tolerance and respect for the value of our national inheritance that distinguished it, on the one hand, from the nihilism of continental revolutionaries, and on the other, from those in the political class who have forgotten (or never learned) the history of their country. When zealots came to Attlee to demand the abolition of the House of Lords, his very brief, pragmatic and very English response was to leave it alone: 'it works'.[10]

William Bagehot was one of the most incisive minds to reflect upon these peculiarities of the English. Not only a prodigious historian, he was also a great proponent of what he saw as our evolutionary constitution. He explained that power could relocate itself into existing institutions. Bagehot significantly entitled his great book *The English Constitution*.

Bagehot and political power on the move

Bagehot was a journalist of great distinction who edited *The Economist*. But it is not for his editorial skills that Bagehot is best remembered. His fame primarily comes from a series of nine essays published in the *Fortnightly Review* between 1865 and 1867. Each dealt with an aspect of the unwritten constitution – the Monarchy, the House of Lords, the House of Commons, on changes of government, on checks and balances in this informal system and reflections on its history. He gathered these essays into a single volume, publishing *The English Constitution* in 1867.

This volume is a monument to Bagehot at his best, revealing him to be one of the most original political observers of his day and beyond. Bagehot was not much interested in the doings of those who exercised political power. Much more important, Bagehot thought, was the recording of those institutions through which power was exercised, and how the hierarchy of institutional importance had changed, was changing, and would continue to change. He was the first writer with wide appeal to focus exclusively on how power within the British constitution had moved from the monarchy, to the great landed interests represented in the Lords, only for the Lords to see power shift in turn to the Commons as the country moved to a universal franchise.

One of Bagehot's other books, less known than his political works, but of seminal importance in understanding the construction of his thinking, traces the relationship between physics and politics. Ten months after the last instalment of *The English Constitution* had appeared in the *Fortnightly Review*, the first of five essays on the prerequisites of what Bagehot called 'verifiable progress' were published. Like most significant intellectuals of that period – such as Karl Marx – Bagehot was much influenced by the publication of Darwin's *On the Origin of Species* in 1859. For us in the early twenty-first century it is fascinating to see so subtle a mind grapple with the dimensions of a new world opening suddenly before him.

Here are the opening lines of Bagehot's *Physics and Politics*, as apt for our situation as they were for his:

One peculiarity of this age is the sudden acquisition of much physical knowledge. There is scarcely a department of science or art, which is the same, or at all the same, as it was 50 years ago. A new world of inventions . . . has grown up around us which we cannot help seeing; a new world of ideas is in the air and affects us, though we do not see it.[11]

Here lies the key to the enduring relevance of Bagehot. Physics is a term for those sciences, which deal with natural phenomena such as motion, force, light and sound. Bagehot rightly saw political power as a force, which was similarly almost impossible to contain in one place, let alone in one organisation, on a permanent basis. Politics is never static. The picture Bagehot painted, of political power on the move between the great institutions of state, was an accurate one in the Victorian age. It has remained relevant to Britain until relatively recently.

Power has migrated since Bagehot wrote, first to what Lord Hailsham called 'the elective dictatorship'. This phrase came from a senior politician who was reflecting midway through his career as a cabinet minister. Hailsham coined this phrase to highlight the movement of power from the Commons to the 'elective dictatorship', i.e. the Cabinet. But, as Bagehot would have prophesised, power was not to remain with the executive. It has since departed from London, first to Brussels and more recently to the newly established Parliaments and assemblies of Scotland, Wales and Northern Ireland. The first transfer of power affects the status of the United Kingdom as a nation state. The second impacts on how what remains of the nation state operates. And the two transfers – the two binds – are intertwined. Changes in England's relationships with Scotland, Northern Ireland and Wales will inevitably, but in ways that cannot at this time be foreseen, influence the relationships of all the elements in a disunited Kingdom, with the EU.

Both relocations of power have been disputed, as was surely the case when the monarch gradually conceded power to the House of Lords, before it moved on again to the House of Commons, and thence to the Cabinet. And, as I have just noted, power has been on the move again, this time to Brussels.

The West Lothian Question

How might Bagehot have seen the devolution of sovereignty to the different parts of the UK? In the early days of devolution, in 1977, Tam Dalyell, Labour MP for the Scottish constituency of West Lothian, posed what has since become known as the West Lothian

Question. Once some power has been conceded to a Scottish Parliament, how could Scottish Members of the UK Parliament continue to vote on issues from which their constituents were exempt? That was the question to which he, and now a growing body of the English electorate, are still waiting for an answer.

In my view, Bagehot would add that such a flagrant mismatch carries within it dangers deeper and wider than itself: for it tears at the legitimacy of Parliamentary representative democracy. It so distorts the balance in the functions of Parliament that it risks stoking the fire of street politics and all the dangers that this involves.

The issue initially carried little weight because, prior to establishing a Scottish Parliament, devolution could only be discussed at a purely theoretical level and, as Orwell notes, the English in particular have never been much interested in theory. In stark contrast, today, the debate is about the practical results of the first stage of devolution and those practical consequences are seen, in part, in the inequitable treatment of English constituents as opposed to the constituents of Scottish MPs. The English voter still has to grasp the true significance of the second front opened in the devolution debate, namely the drive for Scottish Independence pursued by Alex Salmond, the leader of the Scottish National Party (SNP).

Devolution affects English voters and taxpayers in two respects. First, there are the inequities in the provision of services that Scottish devolution has brought about. There are the inequities in health treatment, and who covers the cost of personal care. Students at any university in England and Wales are paying substantial fees, accumulating as a burden of debt to be repaid after graduation. In Scotland, higher education is provided for free.

How do Scottish taxpayers get such a good deal compared to their English compatriots? The answer is very simple. It is a product of the 'Barnett Formula' – so named after Joel Barnett (now Lord Barnett), Chief Secretary to the Treasury under the Labour government of 1974–9. This 'formula' – which Lord Barnett himself denounced in 2010 as unfair – channels centrally collected British tax revenue disproportionately to the Scots. Figures released by the House of Commons library for the year 2010–11 show that, on average, the UK Government spends £1,531 more per head in Scotland than it does in England.

Worse still are the inequalities in the exercise of power in the UK Parliament. In an essay of 1861, Walter Bagehot highlighted another aspect of our politics centring on what he called 'the unseen work of Parliament'. Like *The English Constitution*, this venerable analysis is as fresh today as when it was first published, and its message warns plainly of the danger that the mishandling of devolution has created. Bagehot starts out by reporting that some people had complained that the legislative programme for 1861 seemed rather dull: 'they have wished for something more exciting. . .'[12]

But they were missing half the point of Parliament, Bagehot explained. For sure, it was there to pass laws but 'the first part of the duty of Parliament is the choice of the cabinet, who are to administer the affairs of the country.' Here we can see how Parliament has lost ground to the Executive. There is a sad ring to his spirited description of that atrophied role: 'Burke said that the end of the British constitution was to bring 12 men to the jury box; it will be truer to say that it was to bring 15 good men into a dingy room in Downing Street' (or 22, with a further 10 ministers who are allowed to attend nowadays). And that was but the half of it. For Bagehot went on to spell out Parliament's other role. Because we have so lost sight of this, it merits quoting at length:

Again, Parliament has a function of its own which is distinct from legislation, which in the present state of the world is at least as important. It has an expressive function. An immense and most miscellaneous mass of topics are brought before the English nation every year; the stupendous growth of our trade, the extension of our Empire, the increase of our philanthropy, the refinement of our public spirit, and an augmented national intelligence, increase these subjects year by year. On all these it has an opinion, and it needs an organ for expressing it. Parliament is that organ'.[13]

He ends by reminding us that of course he in no way belittles the legislative duty; but stresses the importance of the expressive duty, not least because a Parliament that is deaf to the voice of the people, and which does not serve as the forum for discussion of their high matters is likely to make bad laws. What matter could be greater than the very existence of the Union? Would the Devolution laws, which have caused our current constitutional melee, have been passed if the expressive functions had been properly activated?[14]

It is here, in these modern departures from sound practice that we begin to see the birth of what can simply be called the politics of the English question. In 1977, Tam Dalyell posed that potent question to Scottish MPs: what right did they have to vote on issues, which only affected English constituents? In similar fashion, my Birkenhead constituents do not believe it is fair that they should face constitutional discrimination, as well as meeting additional costs, which identical people in Scotland do not face. The inequities in the present system are not defensible and need to be addressed.

Power moving between political parties

There is another force at work making a settlement to the English Question more likely, and this also relates to Bagehot's analysis pinpointing the mobility of political power. In Bagehot's lifetime, two recognisable political parties became established and began to compete for power from a growing electorate. Part of his brilliance was to notice that, as these parties were establishing themselves to act as the agents through which our ideas of representative and responsible government would operate, political power was on the move between the institutions through which these political parties would exercise power.[15]

Decades after Bagehot's death, political power moved yet again. But this time, not between the great institutions of state, but between political parties. It determined the fate of the Liberal Party that had failed fully to come to terms with a growing enfranchisement of the working class. Labour leaders responded, reluctantly at first, to the Liberal Party's inability to represent the Labour interest more comprehensively. In the end they formed their own political party. Parties that consistently disappoint their core vote are liable to wither and die, although the dying might be disguised for a time by that core vote wishing to register its protest against the actions of a competing party in power.

Labour stands poised at a similar juncture to that occupied by the Liberals prior to 1918. Labour has failed to represent its core on the English Question. To speak of 'One Nation' is not enough. One must act for it.

Bagehot with hindsight

It is not difficult to make an informed guess as to how Bagehot would have prophesised the transfer of power from London to the constituent countries of the UK. Bagehot, I am sure, would have expected the constitutional gatherings and conventions, and other similar activities that preceded the first great devolution Act (Scotland Act, 1998), to have been extended to England. The surprise he would most probably have registered at such a turn of events, with the political elite excluding the major part of the UK from discussions that would affect it, would, I believe, have been accompanied by a stark warning. In fact I am sure of it, as I re-read his account of Parliament's unseen work. There would be one probable outcome for stifling equitable devolution. Bagehot's whole thesis was that power moved peacefully and naturally over time from one institution to another. Interrupt that free flow and the outcome was likely to be political strife.

In encouraging new areas of debate in the House of Commons, Speaker Weatherill, who served from 1983 to 1992, was always at pains to explain his intentions. He did not want to be acclaimed as a great reforming speaker. His motives were more fundamental: debates excluded from the House of Commons were likely to be conducted and decided upon by extra-Parliamentary bodies. In short, he understood intuitively what Bagehot called the expressive function of parliament. His cautious approach should be applied to the English question. The continued resolution to exclude England from the evolving politics of devolution is likely to lead to the English Question being taken outside Parliament for discussion.

Bagehot would see our current politics as a time of great excitement, an excitement deriving very largely from power once again beginning to move. A move that might again go against either one of the two great parties. As discontent against the Conservative leadership mounts it will be tempting for it to start to play the English Question. Many Labour strategists would like to keep the English question off the political agenda. But for the Tories to claim the English crown could be fatal for Labour. With Labour's current political weakness in England, it would likely never recover from such a move. If Labour is to persuade a largely sceptical English electorate that it is they who speak for England, it must act quickly and boldly.

Of course such a strategy will not be easily accomplished. It will also hold dangers. But failure to stake a pre-emptive and possibly dominant claim to the English inheritance will do nothing but hand it to the Conservatives. Worse, it could threaten Labour's very existence as a major political force. It would be like history repeating, mirroring the fall of the Liberal Party eclipsed by Labour because of its strategic failure to represent the newly enfranchised working class.

Seventy years ago, George Dangerfield wrote his bestselling book *The Strange Death of Liberal England*. To concede the English Question to others because, in the short-term, that is the easiest course of action, could lead a future historian to write The Unnecessary

Death of Labour England. No matter how uncomfortable and challenging, we of the Left must act to keep such a book firmly in the realms of fantasy.

Conclusion

Britain has successfully experienced major transfers of political power over the last 200 years in ways that our Continental neighbours were unable to emulate. For them such dramatic changes involved bloody revolution. By contrast, in Britain, our political institutions remained stable while power moved.

However, ominously, the stable working of our political institutions has changed on two fronts. The way that the British were sold a false bill of goods by Edward Heath's Conservative government has increasingly poisoned our relationships with our continental neighbours. This has been a huge loss to us and, I believe, to them as well. It has also poisoned public trust in a political class, which for too long continued to argue that EU membership was purely about improving our trade relations. One great prize in British politics will go to whichever of the main parties has the courage and imagination to shape a new, more equal relationship with our European neighbours. It should start from the belief that we are a European country, but also a European island, which gives us a political and military culture very different from our mainland neighbours.

The other great change is the way that senior politicians of all parties have dealt with the issue of devolution. It has resulted in an abrupt rupture of the workings of the unwritten constitution which Bagehot described more clearly than anyone, and which worked so well, for so long. Devolution may have been successful in heartening constituent parts to the UK by devolving considerable powers to Scotland, Wales and Northern Ireland. But in this age of the rise of new nation states, the English are beginning to voice legitimate demands to assert their identity. Not to meet these requests within the Parliamentary process, not to reactivate the expressive role Parliament has to play for the people, not to regain their trust, not to reignite the zeal and the courage of Parliamentarians to carry out that role risks handing the issue to non-Parliamentary forces. The likely results of allowing such a scenario to develop are more than frightening.

Notes

1 See Lee. S., *Best for Britain: The Politics and Legacy of Gordon Brown* (2007; London: Oneworld Publications). Possibly the worst offender on this score has been Gordon Brown detailed particularly in his section on 'the conflation of England with Britain', pp.145–9.
2 Bagehot, W., *The English Constitution* (1867; London: Chapman and Hall).
3 Anderson, B., *Imagined Communities: Reflections on the Origin and Spread of Nationalism* (1983; London: Verso).

4 Colley, L., *Britons: Forging the Nation 1707–1837* (1992; Yale: Yale University Press, Yale), p.5.

5 Burke, E., *Reflections on the Revolution in France* (1790; London: Dodsley).

6 McFarlane, A. 'The Origins of English Individualism: Some Surprises', *Theory and Society,* Vol. 6, issue 2, pp.255–77. Roger Scruton has an excellent chapter on the evolution of the Common Law in England in Scruton, R., *England: An Elegy* (2006; London: Continuum).

7 Adamson, J., *The Noble Revolt: The Overthrow of Charles I* (2007; London: Weidenfeld and Nicolson).

8 Orwell, G., *The Lion and the Unicorn: Socialism and the English Genius* (1941). Reprinted in *Collected Essays, Journalism and Letters,* Vol. 2 (1980; Harmondsworth: Penguin), p.119.

9 Ibid., p.12.

10 There does however come a time when even the 'it works' response leaves an institution open to reform if it strongly offends a country's feelings of decency.

11 Bagehot, W., *Physics and Politics* (1872). Reprinted in St John-Stevas, N. (ed.), *The Collected Works of Walter Bagehot,* Vol VII (1965: London: Economist). p. 17.

12 Bagehot, W., *The Unseen Work of Parliament* (1861). Reprinted in St John-Stevas, N. (ed), op. cit., Vol. VI, p.45.

13 Ibid., p.47.

14 I should mention that it was the editor of Walter Bagehot's *Collected Works* (in twelve volumes), the late Norman St John-Stevas, who, as a Conservative Leader of the House, was responsible for the introduction of the modern Select Committee system, a potent innovation that has helped to make a first important move to pull back some powers from the Executive by giving MPs powers to begin, again, to hold the Executive to account before the representatives of the people.

15 By far and away the best text on the development of political ideas on these two concepts, and how they influence our understanding of what political democracy means in this country, is to be found in Birch, A. H., *Representative and Responsible Government* (1964; London: George Allen and Unwin).

Part IV

Cosmopolitanism and Its Discontents

Michael Lind

– 7: What is Wrong with the Cosmopolitan Project? –

T wo decades ago it was often asserted that the end of the Cold War had brought about a collapse of utopian hopes and the discrediting of grand narratives. But what has been called 'the new cosmopolitanism' is a utopian grand narrative, if ever there was one – and it is alive and kicking. Like Marxist socialism, in both its Leninist and democratic varieties, cosmopolitanism, at least in some versions, combines a theory of historical progress with a program for political action to bring about a better world.[1] The secular creed of the new cosmopolitanism comes in several denominations, including democratic peace theory, championed by the American international relations theorist Michael Doyle among others, so-called humanitarian intervention or liberal imperialism, advocated by thinkers and activists including Gareth Evans and Michael Ignatieff, as well as more radical proposals for global government or world federalism like those of the World Federalist Movement.[2] These three schools of thought are united by two things: a belief in a global society of individuals, and a desire to transcend the limits of traditional liberal internationalism.

The rejection of traditional liberal internationalism

follows from ethical cosmopolitanism, because the moral ideal of a global society of individuals is hard to square with the institutions and practices of a global society of states. One of the great services of the mid-twentieth century 'English School' of international relations theory of Martin Wight, Hedley Bull and others was to distinguish a system of states from a society of states, in opposition to conventional realists for whom states exist and interact in a legal and moral void. According to the English School, a mere system of states exists wherever political entities interact, even if they do so in a moral and political vacuum, like the Roman Empire in its interactions with the Parthian Empire. In contrast, according to the English School, the European society of states, and the global society of states which succeeded it under the auspices first of the League of Nations and then of the United Nations, have been societies of states as well as systems of states. A society of states is more than an anarchy, in which no shared norms would exist. But it is also less than a polity, as there is no central power responsible for enforcing such norms. The absence of a sovereign does not mean the absence of law. But in a society of states, law must be enforced as a matter of self-help by member states, alone or in alliance or concerts of power.

It is important to make this distinction because many of the new cosmopolitans, and not a few academic realists, tend to caricature 'the Westphalian system' as an anarchy of states rather than a society of states.

By the way, the term Westphalian is in itself misleading. The modern global society of states was founded in 1945 by the United Nations Charter, not in 1648 by the Treaty of Westphalia, and many of its norms, such as prohibitions on wars of conquest and annexation, are quite different from those of the European state system that preceded it.

To their caricature of the Westphalian system cosmopolitan writers frequently add a caricature of the traditional nation state as an oppressive regime that combines the xenophobic, exclusive nationalism of Nazi Germany with the autarkic economics of North Korea. These caricatures permit many of the new cosmopolitans to claim that increases in cross-border collaboration, trade or immigration, or growing respect for different cultures abroad or minorities at home, are evidence that the intolerant, parochial nation state system of the past is crumbling and giving way to a new and more humane and enlightened post-national order.

Such arguments would have puzzled the patron saints of liberal internationalism and liberal nationalism, like Guiseppe Mazzini, John Stuart Mill, William Ewart Gladstone, Woodrow Wilson, and the two Roosevelts, Theodore and Franklin D. All of them believed that national self-determination, international law, and international cooperation in security and economic affairs were not only compatible, but mutually reinforcing. Trade treaties, liberal immigration policies, cultural exchanges and trans-national NGOs have usually been welcomed by liberal internationalists, even though they reject layers of government above the nation state.[3]

Even less convincing is the claim that there is an innate conflict between human rights and national sovereignty. To be sure, there are illiberal nation states, just as there are illiberal non-national states. But from John Locke through the American Founders and the French revolutionaries to the drafters of the United Nations Human Rights Charter, most champions of universal human rights have taken it for granted that those rights must be secured by particular local communities, which may be nation states but could also be rights-respecting multinational states, regional federations or city states.

The thesis that humanity ought to be divided among independent states that are answerable to self-governing peoples raises the question of how sovereign states are to relate to each other. The two possibilities, as I have already noted, are an anarchy of states and a society of states. Most republican liberals have favored some kind of society of states with common rules and customs. But even at its most institutionalised, the society of states must always fall short of anything resembling a state itself. For liberal internationalism, it is acceptable for political borders to be ethical borders as well. Peoples, and the states that represent them, may have duties to other communities as well as to foreign individuals who fall into the scope of their power. But the duties of particular individuals to other individuals across borders are limited at best, compared to their duties to other members of their own communities. For this reason liberal internationalists tend to be comfortable with inter-governmental institutions but wary of supra-national or trans-national agencies, as potentially incompatible with the self-government of particular peoples. For example, traditional liberal internationalists have been wary of creating supra-national courts that are accountable to no country in particular. At the same time, they seldom object to incorporating international norms, like human rights conventions, into domestic law to be enforced by domestic courts.

The desire to erode or eliminate the distinction between domestic society and international society is shared by otherwise different variants of cosmopolitan thinking. This was the judgement of Martin Wight long before the rise of today's new cosmopolitanism. In the mid-twentieth century he wrote:

The essential characteristic of Revolutionist theory is that it assimilates international relations to a condition of domestic politics. The more international society is conceived of as a civitas maxima, the more international relations will be conceived as the domestic politics of the universal civitas. There are three possible ways of trying to bring about this assimilation: doctrinal uniformity, doctrinal imperialism, and cosmopolitanism.[4]

As an example of doctrinal uniformity as a method of promoting a global society of individuals, Wight cites Kant's essay on 'Perpetual Peace', with its proposed league of states that must have republican constitutions.[5] It is worth noting that Wight does not accuse either the League of Nations or the United Nations of being revolutionist, because both have been open to sovereign states with various kinds of governments.

To illustrate his category of doctrinal imperialism, Wight cited the imposition of French ideas of the rights of man on countries conquered by revolutionary France and Soviet communism. If he had lived he might have included the triumphalism of American neoconservatives in the post-Cold War period.

Wight's third approach to collapsing the distinction between domestic and international politics is cosmopolitanism, which, he says, 'rejects the idea of a society of states and says that the only true international society is one of individuals.' Wight notes that at the level of theory, cosmopolitanism is less important than doctrinal uniformity or doctrinal imperialism, because it gets rid of international relations altogether. 'However,' he says, 'in practice it is influential.'[6]

Although Wight died in 1972, there is very little in the writing of the new cosmopolitan thinkers that does not fit into one or another of his three categories. His category of doctrinal uniformity would include today's democratic peace theory.

Another, less familiar variant of doctrinal uniformity as a version of cosmopolitanism is what might be called cosmopolitan peace theory. Something like this is the ideal described by the German sociologist Ulrich Beck:

A political response to globalisation is the 'cosmopolitan state' which opened itself up to the world. This state does not arise through the dissolution or supersession of the national state, but instead through its inner transformation, through *internal globalisation*. [emphasis in original]. The legal, political, and economic potentialities found at the national and local levels are reconfigured and opened up. This hermaphroditic creature – simultaneously a cosmopolitan and a national state – does not delimit itself nationalistically against other nations. Instead, it develops a network on the basis of mutual recognition of otherness and of equality among difference in order to solve transnational problems. Meanwhile, sovereignty is expanded in order to solve national problems. The concept of the cosmopolitan state is based on the principle of national indifference towards the state. It makes possible the side-by-side existence of various national identities by means of the principle of constitutional tolerance within and of cosmopolitan rights without.

In the wake of the Treaty of Westphalia in 1648, the civil war of the 16th century – which had been shaped by religion – was concluded via the separation of the state from religion. Quite similarly (and this is my thesis) the national world (civil) wars of the 20th century could be concluded by the *separation of state from nation*. [emphasis in original].[7]

If I understand Beck correctly, he is not arguing

for redrawing borders or adding new layers of formal government above today's existing nation states. Instead, what he and others like Jürgen Habermas, who has argued for what he calls 'constitutional patriotism,' seem to have in mind is a revolution in consciousness within today's existing nations, one individual at a time.[8] If I am not mistaken, this is also the implication of the 'rooted cosmopolitanism' promoted by Mitchell Cohen, Bruce Ackerman, Kwame Anthony Appiah and others.[9] They combine calls for enlarging concentric circles of individual awareness and sympathy with a lack of interest in projects like world federalism that would restructure the international community. Even Martha Nussbaum, one of the best known thinkers of the new cosmopolitans, might fit into this category, because her emphasis is on the transformation of the consciousness of individuals, who legitimately can be partial to kin and neighborhood and country, as long as they show more concern for the fates of foreigners than most people do today.[10]

If rooted cosmopolitanism means that we have duties to others beyond national borders, albeit duties that are discounted with distance, then it seems indistinguishable from enlightened patriotism or enlightened nationalism. Only the most chauvinistic nationalists would reject the propositions that all people deserve respect or that one should try to enlarge one's horizons by understanding different cultures and traditions.

The second approach to erasing the distinction between domestic and international society that Wight identifies is what he calls doctrinal imperialism. In the last few decades a version of this approach took the form of so-called liberal or humanitarian imperialism. This school held that we have a moral duty, and not merely a practical interest, in sometimes using military power to aid people in other countries, not only to avert genocide, but also, perhaps, to topple tyrants like Saddam Hussein in Iraq or to bring functioning central government to chaotic territories like Afghanistan.

As these examples demonstrate, blurring the distinction between international law and domestic law practically requires wars of 'regime change' or 'decapitation' – the removal, by means including assassination, of the enemy head of state. Redefining a foreign government as nothing more than a gang of criminals who should be removed from power and, in some cases, arrested and put on trial, tends to delegitimise other options of traditional statecraft, like waging a limited war for limited purposes while leaving the leaders of the enemy state in power. If the local opposition is not capable of forming a functioning government once a tyrant has been deposed by outside forces, then the intervening nations may be confronted, as in Iraq and Afghanistan, with unpalatable choices. They would either have to tolerate famine, anarchy and rampant crime caused by the chaos, which they themselves have created. Or they would have to opt for prolonged occupations in which the foreign forces attempt to govern a country until a native government is capable of exercising sovereignty.

Now that the liberated in Iraq have expelled their American liberators, and that Americans and their allies find they have overstayed their welcome in Afghanistan, the proponents of liberal imperialism have fallen quiet. But this is a perennial theme and it may be revived again in different, more favorable circumstances.

Before leaving this topic, I would like to touch upon the recently-fashionable doctrine of R2P or 'responsibility to protect'. The basic idea, that legitimate states should secure the basic rights of their citizens, is shared by both liberal cosmopolitan imperialists and liberal internationalists. And to the extent that liberal internationalism holds that the modern global system is a society of states, not a mere anarchy of states, then on purely liberal internationalist grounds one could make a case for unilateral or collective intervention by well-organised states to help build legitimate and competent governments capable of protecting their citizens and joining the larger world society. In deciding whether to undertake such risky interventions, liberal internationalists no doubt would weigh the costs and benefits to their own nations more than liberal imperialists or humanitarian hawks.

The third category, which Martin Wight simply called cosmopolitanism, might more accurately be called world federalism, particularly if we see it along with democratic peace theory and liberal imperialism as one of three variants of liberal cosmopolitanism.[11] 'The demand for a world parliament is at last acquiring some serious political muscle,' the British journalist George Monbiot wrote in the *Guardian* in 2007. 'The campaign for a UN parliamentary assembly is being launched this week on five continents. It is backed by nearly 400 MPs from 70 countries, a long and eclectic list of artists and intellectuals – among them Günter Grass, Karlheinz Stockhausen, Alfred Brendel and Arthur C. Clarke . . .'[12] It may not be irrelevant to note that the late Arthur C. Clarke was a science fiction writer, while the late Karlheinz Stockhausen claimed that he was an extraterrestrial from a planet orbiting the star Sirius and described the 9/11 attacks as the greatest work of art in human history.

World federalism is nothing new. If we do not count pre-modern notions of universal empire or universal religious community as precedents, the idea of a parliament of free peoples goes back at least to Enlightenment philosophes like Volney. In *The Rights of Man* (1791), Tom Paine wrote: '[M]y country is the world, and my religion is to do good.'[13] Few discussions of world federalism, by proponents and critics alike, refrain from quoting Tennyson's lines in 'Locksley Hall,' and I will not break with precedent:

> For I dipt into the future, far as human eye could see,
> Saw a Vision of the world, and all the wonder that would be; . . .

Till the war-drum throbb'd no longer, and the battle-flags
    were furled
In the Parliament of man, the Federation of the world.

There the common sense of most shall hold a fretful
    realm in awe,
And the kindly earth shall slumber, lapt in universal
    law.[14]

In 1906, the New York Peace Society, headed by Andrew Carnegie, was founded, and gave rise to subsidiary organisations such as the World-Federation League and the League to Enforce Peace.[15] In 1947, five groups – Americans United for World Government, World Federalists, Massachusetts Committee for World Federation, Student Federalists and World Citizens of Georgia – came together in North Carolina to form the United World Federalists For World Government With Limited Powers Adequate to Prevent War (UFW).[16] It is my impression that nowadays there are fewer supporters of world government in North Carolina and Georgia, if not Massachusetts.

In the early twentieth century, the United States was held up by world federalists as a model for a future united world. This was a false parallel. The inhabitants of Texas and California do not belong to different nations, whatever they may believe. The secession of the South in 1861, followed by what we Southerners call the Late Unpleasantness, was an attempt by a selfish regional oligarchy to preserve its power and privileges, not a bid for independence by a distinct ethno-cultural nation.

Today world federalism tends to have a distinctly anti-American cast, because it is viewed as a way of replacing or limiting American hegemony. The European Union, rather than the USA, is cited as the model of the cosmopolitan world federation of the future. For example, Ulrich Beck describes Europe as 'a cosmopolitan federation of states, which cooperates in order to tame economic globalisation while ensuring recognition of the otherness of the Other (meaning the European co-nations, but also Europe's neighbours worldwide) . . .'

Whether or not the European Union has succeeded in recognising 'the otherness of the Other' I will leave to others, if not the Other, to decide. The EU clearly falls short not merely of a federal state but even of a workable confederation like Switzerland. As people around the world have learned recently, Europe has a currency union but not the fiscal union or transfer union necessary to make a currency union work. And most of what William Blackstone and Jean Bodin called 'the marks of sovereignty' such as military policy and social insurance remain with Europe's constituent nation states.

Whether it is considered a success, a failure or a work in progress, Europe's experiment in partial pooling of national sovereignty is not being emulated anywhere else in the world. NAFTA, MERCOSUR and

ASEAN are nothing but limited multilateral trading zones. Populists in Canada, Mexico and the United States alike live in dread of the appearance of anything resembling a North American Union. No multilateral regional institutions comparable to the EU or NATO link Japan, the Koreas and China, or unite India and Pakistan with the smaller states of South Asia. The post-colonial societies in Africa and the Middle East and Latin America are deeply jealous of their sovereignty.

Unable to point to any trend outside of Europe toward the surrender of sovereignty to decision-making bodies higher than the nation state, proponents of world federalism sometimes claim that global government must inevitably follow the creation of a global society by the global market. But we have heard this before – ever since 1848, in fact, when Marx and Engels published the communist manifesto:

The bourgeoisie has through its exploitation of the world-market given a cosmopolitan character to production and consumption in every country . . . All old-fashioned national industries have been destroyed or are daily being destroyed . . . In place of the old wants, satisfied by the productions of the country, we find new wants, requiring for their satisfaction the products of distant lands and climes. In place of the old local and national seclusion and self-sufficiency, we have intercourse in every direction, universal inter-dependence of nations.[17]

The bourgeoisie have had 164 years to replace nationalism with cosmopolitanism and they do not seem to have gotten very far. Every generation since 1848, there have been more nation states than before. In spite of all the chatter about the global market and the triumph of laissez-faire capitalism, in the last few decades, three of the four major industrial nations – China, Japan, and Germany – have been classic mercantilist nations that rigged their domestic economic institutions and currency policies to produce perpetual trade surpluses for their national export industries. The United States and Britain, I should add, have practised mercantilism, too, but in the interest of finance rather than manufacturing. The ambition to be the world's financial centre in a zero-sum competition drove deregulation in both the City of London and Wall Street, on the thoroughly nationalistic theory that what was good for the country's bankers was good for the country.

It may be some time before 'the battle flags are furled' 'and the kindly earth shall slumber, lapt in universal law', to speak with Tennyson. Millennial hopes for the transcendence of international rivalry by means of world government have tended to be greatest at the end of world wars. If we think of the Cold War as the third world war of the twentieth century, a world war fought indirectly by means of embargos, arms races, proxy wars and propaganda, then it is hardly surprising that its conclusion should have been followed in the 1990s and 2000s by a revival of hope that the end of a particular great-power conflict would be followed by the end of great-power conflict for all time. As the years passed after World War I and World War II, disillusionment took its toll on the world federalist movements, and today's supporters of a global parliament are likely to dwindle in numbers as the euphoria that followed the fall of the Berlin Wall recedes into the past.

The inevitable failure of the cosmopolitan project – whether in the forms of democratic peace theory, liberal imperialism or world federalism – should be welcomed rather than lamented by those of us in the tradition of liberal internationalism. Its ideal, as I have stressed repeatedly, is a civilised society of states accountable to their people and policed by a loose concert of great powers, not an Orwellian struggle among totalitarian regimes.

At the level of ethical theory, Adam Smith in 'The Theory of Moral Sentiments' (1759) defended the legitimacy of particularism in a passage that cannot be improved upon:

Whatever interest we take in the fortune of those with whom we have no acquaintance or connection, and who are placed altogether out of the sphere of our activity, can produce only anxiety to ourselves without any manner of advantage to them…All men, even those at the greatest distance, are no doubt entitled to our good wishes, and our good wishes we naturally give them. But if notwithstanding they should be unfortunate, to give ourselves any anxiety upon that account seems to be not part of our duty. That we should be but little interested, therefore, in the fortune of those whom we can neither serve nor hurt, and who are in every respect so very remote from us, seems wisely ordered by nature . . .[18]

At the level of political theory, it is hard to disagree with Goldwin Smith, professor of modern history at Oxford, who wrote in 1860:

If all mankind were one state, with one set of customs, one literature, one code of laws, and this state became corrupted, what remedy, what redemption would there be? None, but a convulsion, which would rend the frame of society to pieces, and deeply injure the moral life which society is designed to guard. Not only so, but the very idea of political improvement might be lost, and all the world might become more dead than China. Nations redeem each other. They preserve for each other principles, truths, hopes, aspirations, which, committed to the keeping of one nation only, might, as frailty and error are conditions of man's being, become extinct forever. [19]

'. . . [A]ll the world might become more dead than China.' As a symbol of stagnant uniformity, pre-modern imperial China was invoked by Smith's contemporary Tennyson in 'Locksley Hall.' I have already quoted the lines that have inspired several generations of world federalists: 'Till the war-drum throbb'd no longer, and the battle-flags were furl'd/ In the Parliament of man, the Federation of the world.' Those of us who prefer a pluralist world of sovereign nations to a cosmopolitan world order in any form can take inspiration from other, China-inspired verses in the same poem by Tennyson: 'Thro' the shadow of the globe we sweep into the younger day; /Better fifty years of Europe than a cycle of Cathay.'

Notes

1 The literature of the new cosmopolitanism is vast and diverse. See Pogge, T., 'Cosmopolitanism,' in Robert Goodin, R., Pettit, P., and Pogge, T. (eds), *A Companion to Contemporary Political Philosophy* (2007; Oxford: Blackwell), pp.312–31; Calhoun, C., 'Cosmopolitanism in the modern social imaginary,' *Daedalus*, 137:3 (2008), pp.105–14; Waldron, J., 'What is Cosmopolitan?', *Journal of Political Philosophy*, 8:2 (2000), 227–43.

2 For democratic peace theory, see Doyle, M. W., 'Kant, Liberal Legacies, and Foreign Affairs', *Philosophy and Public Affairs*, 12:3 (Summer 1983), pp.205–35; Doyle, M. W., 'Kant, Liberal Legacies, and Foreign Affairs, Part 2', *Philosophy and Public Affairs*, 12:4 (Autumn, 1983), 323–53. For a defence of humanitarian intervention, see Evans, G., Sahnoun, M., et al., *The Responsibility to Protect: Report of the International Commission on Intervention and State Sovereignty* (2001; Ottawa, Canada: International Development Research Centre).

3 For defences of liberal nationalism, see Miller, D., *On Nationality* (1997; Oxford: Oxford University Press); Tamir, Y., *Liberal Nationalism* (1995; Princeton: Princeton University Press); Lind, M., 'National Good', *Prospect*, October 2000.

4 Wight, M., *International Theory: The Three Traditions*, ed. Wight, G., and Porter, B. (1991; New York: Holmes & Meier,), p. 41.

5 Kant, I., 'Perpetual Peace: A Philosophical Sketch', in Hans Reiss (ed.), *Kant: Political Writings* (1991; Cambridge: Cambridge University Press), pp.93–130.

6 Wight, M., op. cit., p.45.

7 Beck, U., 'A new cosmopolitanism is in the air,' Signandsight. com, 20/11/2007.

8 Habermas, J., 'The Postnational Constellation and the Future of Democracy,' in Max Pensky (ed.), *The Postnational Constellation: Political Essays* (2001; Cambridge: Polity Press), pp.58–112.

9 Cohen, M., 'Rooted Cosmopolitanism', *Dissent*, Fall 1992; Bruce Ackerman, B., 'Rooted cosmopolitanism', *Ethics*, 104:3 (1994), 516–35; Appiah, K. A., *Cosmopolitanism: Ethics in a World of Strangers* (2006; New York: W. W. Norton).

10 Nussbaum, M., 'Toward a globally sensitive patriotism', *Daedalus*, 137:3 (2008), 78-93.

11 Archibugi, D.,'Cosmopolitical Democracy', *New Left Review*, 4 (2000), 137–50; Held, D., 'Cosmopolitanism: Globalization Tamed?', *Review of International Studies*, 29 (4).

12 Monbiot, G., 'The best way to give the poor a real voice is through a world parliament', *Guardian*, 23 April 23 2007.

13 Paine, T., *Rights of Man, Common Sense and Other Political Writings* (1998 [1791]; Oxford: Oxford University Press), p.281.

14 Alfred, Lord Tennyson, 'Locksley Hall,' in *Collected Poems* (2007; London: Penguin), pp.51–63..

15 Yoder, J. A., 'The United World Federalists: Liberals for Law and Order' in Chatfield, C. (ed.) *Peace Movements in America* (1973; New York: Schocken), p.112.

16 Ibid., p.114.

17 Marx, K. and Engels, F., *The Communist Manifesto* (1998 [1848]; Oxford: Oxford University Press), p.6.

18 Adam Smith, *The Theory of Moral Sentiments* (2007 [1759]; New York: Cosimo), p.138.

19 Jacob Viner, J., *The Role of Providence in the Social Order: An Essay in Intellectual History* (1972; Philadelphia: American Philosophical Society), p.49.

Garrett Wallace-Brown

– 8: Are States Still Sovereign Actors in the World? –

During the time men live without a common power to keep
them all in awe, they are in that condition called war; and
such a war, as if of every man, against every man.
– Hobbes, *Leviathan*

Without man and his potential for moral progress, the whole
of reality would be a mere wilderness, a thing in vain, and
have no final purpose.
– Immanuel Kant, *Perpetual Peace*

Introduction

A re states still sovereign actors in the world? In
the recent past there have been broadly three
approaches taken when responding to this question.
First, much has been written over the last twenty-
five years about globalisation and the 'hollowing out'
of state sovereignty. For many, the state has become
increasingly 'outdated' and unable to appropriately
respond to the global challenges of the twenty-first
century. Since globalisation has changed the nature
of politics, according to this view, the state must give
way to new forms of global governance. For others,

despite massive changes in its ability to act independently, the state has not evaporated away as quickly and thoroughly as many predicted after the fall of communism. Although some states have clearly buckled under the interconnected strain of the 2008 global financial meltdown, others have faired much better due to prudent self-management and a level of regulatory independence. As a consequence, not only does a level of self-determined sovereignty within a globalised world appear still possible, this capacity is also clearly beneficial to the lives of its citizens. Lastly, there are those who continue to desperately hold onto traditional notions of state sovereignty, arguing that the state is under imminent threat of destruction and that state independence must be protected at all costs, even if this requires states to 'opt out' of existing international treaties and regimes.

In responding to this question, this chapter will defend an intermediate position that seeks to locate compatibility between a cosmopolitan belief in the necessity for strengthened global governance and more neo-sovereigntist positions that continue to demand a return to traditional forms of sovereign independence and self-determination. In doing so, it will be suggested that neo-sovereigntism too narrowly defines what it means to enjoy a sovereign condition. It will argue that a broadened conception of sovereignty can accommodate many of the underlying principles of the neo-sovereigntist critique while also being able to support more legitimate cosmopolitan aspirations for extended global politics.

Nevertheless, unlike other chapters in this volume, which tend to a more practical analysis,[1] this chapter approaches the issue of state sovereignty and cosmopolitan governance in theoretical terms. The reasoning for this is threefold. One, although 'practicality' arguments are important and critics of cosmopolitanism are right to suggest that it often lacks a clear institutional blueprint, this is true of lots of commitments we hold important in our political lives and it would be a fallacy to suggest that just because something is difficult to implement, it is less morally compelling to try and do so. Two, although critics are right to highlight that some cosmopolitans have misguidedly abandoned the state, this is not true of all, for there are many cosmopolitans working to address the very lacuna(s) that critics wrongly accuse them of ignoring.[2] Three, although practical concerns are clearly important within politics, it is also important to reexamine key theoretical debates. In particular, the aim here is to explore whether it is possible for states to be meaningfully 'sovereign' while at the same time being subject to significant external international legal commitments and international institutional governance. If this compatibility can be illustrated as theoretically possible, then it has meaningful relevance to ongoing debates about whether 'states are still sovereign actors in the world.'

Understanding Sovereignty

Traditionally, the concept of state sovereignty has been synonymous with notions of dominion, political authority and self-determination.[3] For an entity to be sovereign, it must enjoy independence from external influence. It must also be able to shape and alter its preferences through a mechanism of self-legislation.

In terms of the history of political thought, we can see this formulation of sovereignty come into being as it develops through the key thinkers of the modern state. For example, in Machiavelli's *Discourses*, sovereignty requires two negative conditions: the freedom from dependence and the power for self-determination. For Machiavelli, sovereignty is defined in largely negative terms, in the sense that it requires independence from external restraint and the ability to reach an internally defined legislated end. Specifically, it must allow for the power to self-determine, self-legislate and, most importantly, to pursue 'reason of state'.[4] This conception of sovereignty is further adopted by Thomas Hobbes in his construction of state authority[5] and was arguably codified into international law by the Treaty of Westphalia. As any introductory textbook will suggest, this conceptualisation of sovereignty has remained the philosophical underpinning of international law and International Relations ever since.

As a result, it is important to note that this traditional notion of sovereignty is deeply entrenched in our thinking about global politics. Contemporary discussions in International Relations often still cluster around 'state right', self-determination and the state's capacity to enjoy legal and political sovereignty from outside influence. However, these debates tend to be pursued based on a rather negative, narrowly zero-sum, and generally unsophisticated conception of state sovereignty as an ideal condition of self-determined independence. This is certainly true in the growing arguments made by neo-sovereigntists.

Neo-sovereigntists, self-determination and the importance of the state

During the last fifteen years there have been renewed calls for states to resist global legal and political regimes that threaten the state's capacity for self-determination. It would seem that global institutions are being increasingly questioned by states that claim that global institutions threaten their ability to be sovereign entities. This position is not just promoted by more authoritarian governments, but is also strongly championed by many intellectuals and policy makers in democratic states.[6] As the former American Ambassador to the United Nations, John Bolton, has recently argued, 'for virtually every area of public policy there is a globalist proposal, consistent with the overall objective of reducing individual nation state autonomy, particularly that of the United States'.[7] As Bolton and the former US Deputy Assistant Attorney General John Yoo suggest, 'America needs to maintain its sovereignty and autonomy, not to subordinate its policies, foreign and domestic, to international control.'[8] The immediate implication of this position is that a certain level of independence and self-determination is both politically mandatory as well as morally justifiable and that expanding global legal and political regimes threaten these critical elements of domestic political life.

This call for the protection of state sovereignty is not a position exclusive to its most radical proponents in the United States.[9] It can be found in equal parts within many debates about Europeanisation and from eurosceptics who employ similar arguments for 'protecting' sovereignty within their arguments against European integration. The implication is that a certain level of state sovereignty is required for democratic self-determination and that the EU immediately threatens this condition. For example, John Strafford, a conservative British politician and author, has recently quoted a renewed 'need to decide whether [Britain] is to remain a democratic nation, governed by the will of its own electorate expressed in its own parliament, or whether it will become a province in a new European superstate under institutions which know nothing of political right and liberties'.[10] This stance can also be witnessed in the various debates about EU legal jurisdiction,[11] about the abdication of state sovereignty to the EU regime,[12] and found within more national-istic positions that question the moral justifiability of increasing the powers or influence of any type of inter-national institution.[13]

In studying these reemerging claims for the pro-tection of state sovereignty, Peter Spiro, an American professor of international law and others have la-beled advocates of such a view as neo-sovereigntists, suggesting that this group of influential scholars and policy makers have had a profound impact on recent international foreign policy and the move away from international cooperation.[14] According to Spiro, neo-sovereigntism holds the position that international institutions and the resulting strengthening of interna-tional law 'trespasses on a nation's core domestic au-thority' and that international institutions promote a 'lawmaking process that is unaccountable' to domestic populations.[15] Because of this, neo-sovereigntism in-sists that democratic states, in particular the US, but also other Western democracies, should be able to 'opt out of international regimes as a matter of power, legal right, and constitutional duty.'[16]

In order to better understand this rather strict conceptualisation of sovereignty, it is beneficial to flesh out two primary claims made by the neo-sovereigntist position. In so doing it can be shown that the current debate is not about state sovereignty per se, but re-lates more to questions of procedural legitimacy at the global level.

The first claim made by neo-sovereigntists involves the notion of institutional accountability. It maintains that international institutions lack acceptable methods to ensure accountability to the citizens of states, and thus would threaten existing domestic accountability chains if more sovereignty were to be abdicated to international regimes. As John Yoo argues, 'international cooperation calls for the transfer of rulemaking authority to international organisations that lack American openness and accountability'.[17] Chris Bradley, a US legal scholar, further suggests that 'by transferring legal authority from US actors to international actors – actors that are physically and culturally more distant from, and not directly responsible to, the US electorate – these delegations may entail a dilution of domestic political accountability.'[18] Implicit in these statements is an appeal to internal checks and balances and a condition of self-help. As such, legal authority gains its normative force through clear channels of deliberation, responsiveness and enforceable accountability measures that can guarantee the legitimacy of rulemaking. Jeremy Rabkin, an American professor of constitutional and international law supports this view, arguing that legal and political accountability requires an exclusive identification relationship between political authority and legal subject, which can only be found in tightly defined constitutional arrangements.[19] Since there is an absence of this relationship at the international level, international organisations that insist

on some meaningful level of political and legal authority are incompatible with the legitimacy provided by
constitutional democracies and the rule of law that
their constitutions protect.[20]

The second claim made by neo-sovereigntists involves the importance of state self-determination and
argues that international institutions generally suffer
from a 'democratic deficit' and thus threaten the self-
determination of democratic peoples.[21] This is particularly worrisome for democratic self-determination,
especially if democratic decisions made domestically
are negated or overturned by international institutions. As Bob Barr, former US federal prosecutor and
former Congressman suggests, 'today, nary a thought is
given when international organisations, like the U.N.,
attempt to enforce their myopic vision of a one-world
government upon America'.[22] As other neo-sovereigntists argue, there is a real possibility for conflicts
to arise between local democratic self-legislation and
institutional decisions at the global level.[23]

These conflicts of jurisdiction and self-determination could present cases where meaningful values
conflict[24] placing the moral 'good' of free democratic
choice against another moral 'good,' such as international environmental regulations which on occasions
may differ from domestic democratic choice. These
potential conflicts are not limited to large-scale issues
of international law, for they can also concern more
mundane and local issues. For example, there is cur-

rently considerable debate within the United Kingdom about whether it should fully comply with all European regulations regarding immigration, trade and EU human rights law. In many of the cases where EU and UK regulations clash, it is claimed that there is a direct conflict between a democratically legislated provision and the regulations demanded by a EU treaty. It is in response to such potential and actual conflicts that many neo-sovereigntists support the right of democratic states to 'opt out' of these international regimes when it can be shown to threaten a sense of legitimate self-determination.[25]

In other words, neo-sovereigntists are deeply concerned about the lack of direct accountability to democratic states and fear that international institutions can (and do) threaten domestic constitutional structures. This position, as we have observed, relies on a particular definition of sovereignty and what it means to 'still be a sovereign actor in the world'. In summary, a state's decision-making should be free from external determination; it should be able to enjoy a very high level of unmolested independence of action, a condition of self-help and self-legislated 'reason of state'. Nevertheless, an alternative conception of sovereignty that is compatible with the neo-sovereigntist position as well as with moderate cosmopolitan aspirations for more robust global governance is conceivable. However, before providing a sketch of this alternative conception it is useful to expose two problematic founding principles inherent within the concept of sovereignty as it has been applied by neo-sovereigntists. I have termed these conditions of 'sovereignty' as the problem of sovereign independence and the problem of sovereignty as isolated self-determination.

The problem of sovereignty as independence

As we have seen, neo-sovereigntists claim that sovereignty requires a significant level of independence and that this need for independence permits states to opt out of international regimes when and where conflicts between the two arise. Nevertheless, it is important to question this assumption when it is presented in its most strict and negative form. For would it always be the case that external dependency threatens an entity's self-determination and institutional integrity? To answer this, it seems fitting that we should consider the example of upholding regulatory sanctions in the international legal system, since these sanctions are claimed to impinge most destructively on the sovereignty of a state. Supposing that the presence of these international sanctions exist (they do) it follows that states would have to have their independence in some sense restricted. The question neo-sovereigntists ask is whether the sovereignty of the state is also limited by complying with these legal commands. A response could be that the absence of independence alone does not always reduce self-determination. For example, 'if the idea of consent, in some form, to the rule of law makes sense, if we can legitimately think of the sanctions as being self-imposed, then autonomy has not been impaired.'[26]

By analogy we can see that to function as a self-determined state actor in this world might actually require dependence and a reduction of independence, in contrast to the traditional negative formulation. Let us take an analogy found in Homer's Odyssey for example. As the story goes, Odysseus, who was serenaded by the sirens, but who did not want to be lured onto the jagged shore, ordered his men to tie him to the mast of his ship and to refuse later orders to set him free. In this case, Odysseus wanted to limit his independence of action, by being dependent on the acts of his men, exactly for the reason that it was the best way to assure survival. In limiting his liberty, in accordance with Odysseus' wishes, his men actually promoted, not hindered, his efforts to determine an outcome of his own choosing. In this regard, self-determination was actually enhanced, despite the fact that he was made dependent on external restraint and a loss of independence.

This leads to an alternative understanding of self-determined sovereignty that can take account of decisions that states and people might actually wish to make in relation to global institutional regulation: in short, a more Kantian inspired conception of what positive self-determination may require. Under this understanding, an entity should have what Kant calls *Willkür*, or the ability to be a 'law onto oneself'.[27] Although a level of independence is a necessary requirement for making a choice, it is not a sufficient condition. An entity, in order to be in some sense autonomous, only requires the 'capacity of choice as the grounds for determining a choice of action'.[28] Nevertheless, if this choice of action resulted from a wish to live interdependently with others, under a system of interest trumping norms or laws, then such a wish would be valid. As long as those laws are understood by an entity as co-legislated 'laws onto oneself', then sovereignty is not abdicated as neo-sovereigntists argue, but is actually facilitated as a self-determining choice of action. As Gerald Dworkin, an American professor of moral, political and legal philosophy suggests, one can limit autonomy for the sake of self-determination itself. There is no logical reason to assume that this act is not representative of a self-determined will.[29]

The problem of sovereignty as isolated self-determination

The second problem with negative definitions of sovereignty is the idea that a condition of 'real' sovereignty is held as one of isolated self-determination. Isolated self-determination suggests that an entity is self-determined if and only if its decisions can be formulated without interference by external conditions. As seen above, neo-sovereigntists are concerned about internal democratic processes, accountability and formulations of self-will in line with constitutional procedures. Since this condition is potentially threatened by international regimes, state self-determination requires a process of self-legislation that is mutually exclusive of this external source. Nevertheless, by treating self-determination as a wholly internal process (without interference or influence), and without reference to law-making communities in which one is in contact with, it actually undermines a significant aspect of what we might wish to derive from the idea of sovereignty. This is because, as the analogy of Odysseus illustrates, we might actually wish to cooperate or rely on others when defining the contours of our lives. Furthermore, as a matter of fact, states have never enjoyed a true sense of independence from foreign influence. The Treaty of Westphalia of 1648, which is often heralded as the legal foundation of self-determined sovereignty, is after all a relational legal construct. Sovereignty represents a way of acting in relation to other states and global bodies. Hence, by its very existence, it opposes any absolute notion of independent self-determination. No matter what more extreme statists, nationalists, conservatives, communitarians and neo-sovereigntists might say – it is not clear that states have ever been sovereign actors in an absolute sense. In this regard, the question is not whether sovereignty represents a condition absent of external influence, but whether an entity can be self-determining while also being highly influenced by external factors.

A Kantian-based cosmopolitan argument would suggest that this is possible. For Kant, self-determination is not conducted within a vacuum and it requires an 'awareness of participating with others in a law making community'.[30] This is because to 'be a law onto oneself' in any social scheme (i.e. any moral or legal community that may have influence on each other), would also necessitate the option to co-legislate as a law-making member in a universal kingdom of ends.[31] This approach to sovereignty sees international cooperation and co-legislation as an expression of self-determined sovereignty rather than a restriction of it. Or in other words, states can enhance their own independence and self-determined will by participating co-operatively with each other through legal and political channels.[32]

Locating legitimacy: state sovereignty as an expression of cosmopolitan willkür

As stated earlier, neo-sovereigntists often claim that the current state of international affairs suffers from a democratic deficit and, as a result, this requires a retreat back to a strong conception of state sovereignty and self-help. Cosmopolitans, on the other hand, believe that an increasingly globalised world requires a positive move away from being solely self-referential, toward a robust commitment to global governance and international institutions. Although cosmopolitan institutional designs vary – they include more reasonable schemes of cosmopolitan democracy[33] versus more radical notions for a world state[34] - most cosmopolitans, if not all, suggest that a transfer of some state autonomy to the global level of some kind will be necessary.[35] As a result, the debate has insipidly persisted as an undernourished presupposition of negative right by both sides.

This is why I believe it is fruitful to explore the idea of sovereignty through a Kantian perspective. Not only does it have positive implications for the ongoing debate about the scope of global governance and the role of states to 'still be sovereign actors in the world'. It also seems to capture something more practical in regards to the actual world we live in, by reconciling issues of international regulation with state self-determination. A Kantian expression of Willkür refocuses the debate away from zero-sum calculations about an entity being or not being self-determined, to issues regarding the procedural legitimacy of self-determined will and its expression in a universal kingdom of ends. This could go some way to satisfy the apprehensions of neo-sovereigntists as well as cosmopolitans. For concerns of self-determination, accountability and the need for stronger global governance might be alleviated when the following conditions for legitimacy can apply (and can be seen to apply) to international regimes. First, a self-determined act of Willkür, as applied to international institutions, stipulates that an entity is sovereign if it has the capacity to be a law unto itself (as expression of will, but not always mutually exclusive of being dependent). Second, institutional self-determination is the capacity to co-legislate as a law-making member in a universal kingdom of ends (as an applied expression of self-will in regards to others, but not necessarily exclusive of external influence).

If we hold these two principles of Willkür as legitimate expressions of sovereign self-will in some meaningful sense, then we can say that more cosmopolitan governance regimes can actually enhance the self-determination of states and the legitimacy of international organisations. This can be said to be accomplished if, and only if, these institutional structures: 1) are deliberative in the sense that they are representative of co-legislation in relation to a mutually consistent kingdom of ends (self-will), and; 2) these institutions are based on mutual public reason in the sense that co-legislation is seen as procedures that can be understood as reasonably accepted by all (laws onto oneself). As an alternative to current understandings, the concern for sovereignty is not limited to its negative form as independence from external restraint, but in its effective form as self-determinism in relation to others. Namely, insuring the capacity for self-determined choice in a mutual system of co-legislation, so that sovereignty truly represents the imposition of 'a law onto oneself'. This takes place within a structure where isolated self-determinism is not only impossible empirically under conditions of globalisation, but also impractical, if self-determinism is to have any expression at the global level.

So how does this reformulated notion of what it means to be a 'sovereign actor in the world' and its corresponding requirements of procedural legitimacy play out against the arguments of neo-sovereigntism and the idea of cosmopolitan global governance? As we have seen, for neo-sovereigntists, international institutions lack acceptable methods to ensure accountability to the citizens of states, and thus, threaten existing accountability chains. In addition, international institutions suffer from a democratic deficit and therefore can conflict with the constitutional authority of states. Conversely, many cosmopolitans claim that global institutions continue to be dominated by a minority of powerful states which act in their own interests, not that of the whole of humankind. As a consequence, they cannot effectively respond to pressing global challenges. Nevertheless, although the arguments of both sides are underpinned by a notion of sovereignty as either a good thing or prohibitive thing, it would seem that the concerns expressed are not actually about sovereignty. If we take their claims at face value, they are about the legitimacy of the system in which sovereignty ought to be expressed. As I have suggested, if we understand sovereignty as a Kantian principle of state Willkür, and if this demands the fulfillment of the two aforementioned legitimacy criteria, then what is needed is not a retreat to isolated sovereignty in its classic Hobbesian formulation, but institutional reform toward a more legitimate international system.

Despite this alternative vision of institutional sovereignty, there is no doubt that most neo-sovereigntists will remain unsatisfied. This is because at the root of the neo-sovereigntist argument is a firm belief that international institutions simply cannot be made accountable in any thoroughgoing sense.[36] In spite of the reality that most international institutions are actually restrained by powerful states and operate within strict mandates,[37] the idea of international institutional accountability is absolutely rejected by neo-sovereigntists as a matter of empirical fact. This in some real sense becomes a self-fulfilling prophecy, where a belief in impossibility drives the very policies that make such a condition impossible. It is perhaps here that cosmopolitans offer a somewhat better vision for coming to terms with issues of globalisation, global interdependence and international legal constitutionalisation. For unlike the neo-sovereigntist position, which also complains that the current order is undemocratic and unaccountable, almost all cosmopolitans concern themselves with issues of procedural fairness, relational legitimacy, democratic participation and institutional justice at the global level. In this regard, cosmopolitans believe that it is not simply enough to say that things are undemocratic and unaccountable – which they do agree that they are – it is also important to suggest institutional designs for how they might not be, especially in a world that is seemingly becoming more interdependent and globalised.

Conclusion

It would seem that negative concepts of sovereignty are significantly entrenched in our thinking about self-determination, international organisations and global governance, which restrictively frame the debate. An alternative reading of sovereignty could reconcile the primary concerns of accountability and self-determination expressed by neo-sovereigntists while also making clear advances toward more legitimate designs for cosmopolitan global governance. It is encouraging to note that reconciliation of communal sovereignty and national sovereignty took place at the domestic level during The Enlightenment – with reasonable success. Although we might still be struggling to approximate a perfect balance domestically, this illustrates, that with time and perseverance, and despite difficulties, such an endeavour is not impossible. If we understand the global level as simply another form of social cooperation that demands a legitimate system of representation by states wishing to express the self-determination of its peoples, and if we are willing to accept that states should act as co-legislators in a global kingdom of ends, then what is required is not a retreat to notions of isolated sovereignty where one can opt out whenever one pleases. Instead, we must reapply at the global level the very principles of institutional legitimacy and expressed self-determination that neo-sovereigntists seemingly hold so dear.

Notes

1 See the critique offered by Michael Lind in this volume.

2 Brown, G. W., 'Bringing the State back into Cosmopolitanism: The Idea of Responsible Cosmopolitan States', *Political Studies Review*, 2011, 9:53.

3 As one popular legal encyclopedia suggests, it refers to 'the supreme, absolute power by which an independent state is governed and from which all specific political powers are derived . . . the intentional independence of a state, combined with the right and power of regulating its internal affairs without external interference or influence.' *Stanford Encyclopedia of Law*.

4 Machiavelli, N., *The Discourses* (1970; London: Penguin), especially Book I, chps 1–10 and 19–23; Book II, chps 6–10 & 19–23; and Book III, chps. 7–9.

5 Hobbes, T., *Leviathan* (1996; Cambridge: Cambridge University Press).

6 This chapter will focus exclusively on democratic states. This is because it is uninteresting to simply observe authoritarian governments and their obvious opposition to any loss of strict state self-determination and the construction of more robust

international regimes. What is more stimulating as well as philosophically challenging is to examine self-determination and issues of sovereignty in democratic states. There, conflicts between internal democratic processes and external global legal commitments may arise. In addition, it is far more arguable that legitimate democratic claims for self-determined sovereignty carry greater moral authority and weight.

7   Bolton, J., 'Should we Take Global Governance Seriously?', *Chicago Journal of International Law*, 2000, Vol. 1, 220. See also J. Bolton, 'Global Governance and Shared Sovereignty', speech given to the American Enterprise Institute for Public Policy Research on 4 April 2008; online at http://www.aei. org/bolton/sharedsovereignty.html (accessed 20 June 2012).

8   Bolton, J., and Yoo, J.,'Restore the Senate's Treaty Power', *New York Times*, 5 January 2009.

9   See arguments presented by Roger Scruton, Daniel Hannan and Frank Field in this volume.

10 Strafford, J., 'Our Fight for Democracy', The Bruges Group, 2009; found at www.brugesgroup.com/index.live. The original quote used by Strafford is by Enoch Powell in 1976.

11 Forster, A., *Eurosceptism in Contemporary British Politics: Opposition to Europe in the British Conservative and Labour Parties Since 1945* (2002; London: Routledge).

12 Taggart, P., and Szczerbiak, A. (eds), *Opposing Europe? The Comparative Party Politics of Euroscepticism*: Vols. 1 & 2, *Comparative and Theoretical Perspectives* (2008; Oxford: Oxford University Press).

13 David Miller, *National Responsibility and Global Justice* (2007; Oxford: Oxford University Press).

14 Peter Spiro, 'The New Sovereigntists', *Foreign Affairs*, 1–5 (December 2000).

15 Ibid.

16 Ibid.

17 Yoo, J., *Powers of War and Peace: The Constitution and Foreign Affairs After 9/11* (2005; Chicago: Chicago University Press), iii.

18 Bradley, C., 'International Delegations, the Structural Constitution, and Non-Self Execution,' *Stanford Law Review*, 55

(2003), 1558.

19 Rabkin, J., *Law without Nations? Why Constitutional Government Requires Sovereign States* (2005; Princeton: Princeton University Press).

20 Rabkin, J., *The Case for Sovereignty: Why the World Should Welcome American Independence* (2004; Cambridge, MA; AEI Press).

21 Barr, Rep. B., 'Protecting National Sovereignty in an Era of International Meddling: An Increasing Difficult Task,' *Harvard Journal on Legislation*, 39 (2002), 323–4.

22 Ibid.

23 Bradley, C., and Goldsmith, J., 'Customary International Law as Federal Common Law: A Critique of the Modern Position,' *Harvard Law Review*, 1997, Vol. 110, p.815.

24 Yoo, J., 'Globalism and the Constitution: Treaties, Non-Self-Execution, and the Original Understanding', *Columbia Law Review*, 99 (1999), 1555.

25 'A Defense of Sovereignty', interview with J. Rabkin, National Review Online, 10 March 10, 2005; available online at http://nationalreview.com/script/comment/rabbkin20050310074 (accessed 20 June 2012).

26 Dworkin, G., *The Theory and Practice of Autonomy* (1988; Cambridge: Cambridge University Press), p.23.

27 Kant, I., *The Grounding for the Metaphysics of Morals* (1981; Indianapolis: Hackett).

28 Ibid, p.38 [4:431-34].

29 G. Dworkin, 'Paternalism', *Monist*, 1972, Vol. 56.

30 Linklater, A., *Men and Citizens in the Theory of International Relations* (2nd edn., 1990; Basingstoke: Macmillan), p.101.

31 Kant, op. cit., p.39 [4:433].

32 Epstein, D., and O'Halloran, S., 'Sovereignty and Delegation in International Organizations', *Law and Contemporary Problems*, 70 (2008); Hathaway, O., 'International Delegation and State Sovereignty', *Law and Contemporary Problems*, 70 (2008); Raustiala, K., 'Rethinking the Sovereignty Debate in International Economic Law', *Journal of International Economic Law*, 6 (2003).

33 D. Held, *Democracy and the Global Order: From the Modern State to Cosmopolitan Governance* (1995; Cambridge: Polity Press).

34 Cabrera, L., *Political Theory of Global Justice: A Cosmopolitan Case for the World State* (2004; New York: Routledge).

35 Unlike the claims made by Michael Lind in this volume, cosmopolitanism has a long tradition with various movements and positions. As a result, not all cosmopolitans advocate a world state or advocate military intervention as he insinuates (I certainly don't advocate either position and I do consider myself cosmopolitan). There are certainly more moderate champions of cosmopolitanism that believe that states are useful political constructions, that national ties do not have to be surrendered, and that cultural plurality is a reason for cosmopolitan universals and not something that has to be rooted out. See respectively, Ypi, L., 'Statist Cosmopolitanism', *Journal of Political Philosophy*, 2008, Vol. 16, 48; K. C. Tan, Justice Without Boarders (2004; Cambridge: Cambridge University Press); and Nussbaum, M., 'Toward a Globally Sensitive Patriotism', *Daedalus*, Summer 2008, p.78.

36 In this regard I believe that many neo-sovereigntists are rather disingenuous in their intentions. This is because they assert strong concerns about democratic choice, accountability and legitimacy, while at the same time making these concepts absolutely dependent on another overriding empirical premise. This premise, it seems to me, comes from classical realism and asserts that we live in an anarchic world where it is more important to maximise state self-interest and power than to be bound to any meaningful rules of the game. However, if this premise acts as the sole background condition for normative theorising, then neo-sovereigntists can dispense with their democratic appeals and simply revert back to the old debates about calculating strategic power and how international institutions can be used as vehicles for exercising this power.

37 Guzman, A., and Landsidle, J., 'The Myth of International Delegation', *California Law Review*, 96 (2008).

Part V

Decline (and Fall?)
of International Governance

Julian Lindley-French

– 9: The Return of State Power: Why the UN and the EU Are Stalling –

> Power is not an institution, and not a structure; neither
> is it a certain strength we are endowed with; it is the name
> that one attributes to a complex strategical situation in
> a particular society.
> – Michel Foucault[1]

Introduction

The United Nations and the European Union are stalling as political projects. Why? On the face of it both institutions appear incapable of dealing with contemporary crises. Indeed, many people think both institutions are not only stalling, but also causing crises – or, at the very least, placing obstacles in the way of their resolution. The reasons are both immediate and profound. There is a lack of understanding, or a lack of willingness to understand, on the part of those at the political heights of both organisations just how and how fast the international system is changing. Both institutions were born of a post-colonial, post-war age when redistributive international politics was in fashion. In the wake of the 2008 economic and financial crash of the West, the relationship between the hitherto 'developed' and 'developing' world has been turned on its head. Institutions designed to reflect power relations of a bygone age and to transfer moneys from the former rich to the emerging rich lack both popular political legitimacy and more fundamentally means.

The stalling of the UN and EU has also prompted the re-emergence of old power in a new guise. Geo-politics is back in fashion and with it the big power state. For institutions such as the UN and EU to function, sound strategy and diplomacy – the twin pillars of effective big picture statecraft – are essential. Both are lacking, replaced instead by process and 'business'. Sadly, in Europe the statecraft that should go hand-in-hand with geopolitics and today's great power politics has been lost. Like a muscle not exercised, an instrument not practiced, this essential skill has simply gone missing. These days, old European powers are so unsure of their right to use might, so bedevilled as they are by the political correctness that eats from within government that constraint becomes in effect paralysis.

At this critical moment in history, even in the act of failing, the UN and especially the EU render Europe today far less than the sum of its parts.

For the first time in 400 years, emerging Asian powers are starting to set the rules of the geopolitical game. In a world in which competitive state power and influence are the currency, a global balance of power is re-emerging. In future years it could either lead to a new bipolar system, built around China and the US, or a concert of powers. Either system will tend to marginalise institutions that are endeavouring to become ends in themselves by ending state power.

Whilst not the same institutions, the UN being global and intergovernmental, the EU regional and a mix of intergovernmental and supranational, both suffer from the two essential contradictions of all collective security mechanisms in the face of great power politics. They face a sovereignty deficit: to function effectively they require the states that invented them to vote themselves out of power. They also create a leadership deficit: as institutions enlarge they first dilute leadership and then tend to fail due to over-representation and the exaggeration of weak state influence. When in an act of desperation, the leadership of a strong state is finally reinforced, it condemns them to fail.

Lessons from history

Both the UN and EU emerged either as institutions (the UN) or as concepts (the EU) at a moment when the European state had been cast into disrepute – 1945 and the end of World War Two. The UN was essentially created by the US because Americans believed Europe to be the crucible of conflict and that Europeans were addicted to war. For the Americans the UN was to be the place where lesser states (everybody else) would be prevented from fighting each other for base reasons whilst the 'shining city on the hill' stood aloof, the real guarantor of world peace. To paraphrase Churchill's famous 1953 comment on the European Defence Community, the US was 'with them but above them'.[2]

American absence, allied to British and French disarmament, had doomed to failure the UN's forerunner in the interbellum, the League of Nations. The US had chosen to opt out of playing the role of Leviathan, which hitherto had been played beyond Europe by Britain and within Europe by a concert of powers – a balance of power.[3] America was not going to make that mistake again. However, there was of course another Leviathan on the block in 1945, the Soviet Union. The UN thus became a platform for two state-centric spheres of influence to compete rather than co-operate.

The EU, on the other hand, or rather its antecedents, the European Coal and Steel Community (ECSC), the European Economic Community (EEC) and the European Community (EC), were created by France and Germany under the auspices of the Americans to remove French and German systemic competition believed to have been at the root of three European wars (1870–71, 1914–18 and 1939–45). All of which had visited immense destruction on the Old Continent. As it evolved, 'Europe' became a mechanism for the rebuilding of a Europe shattered after World War Two. Critically, it was born of the French statist tradition which meant from the beginning Paris saw it as a means not only to constrain German power but to extend French power and influence and thus balance (and exclude) the two 'Anglo-Saxon' powers, America and Britain.

In the early days there were attempts to involve Europe's third great power, Britain, primarily via the European Defence Community between 1952 and 1954. However, the focus of the ECSC was unswervingly on France and Germany with the Benelux countries and Italy effectively add-ons. Moreover, because the ECSC was born of the French statist tradition, the political culture contrasted markedly with that of a more free-market Britain which could at best only ever be semi-attached. Even after joining the EEC in 1973 Britain has never been at the 'heart of Europe' and its relationship with the EU can at best be described as creative political fudge.[4] The Euro-crisis has now revealed that schism for what it is. It is very hard to see how any such posturing can be maintained if a Germany in pursuit of a credible and stable Euro drives the Union towards German-led hybrid-integration.

Churchill's dictum that 'we are with them but not of them' is thus as relevant today for Britain as it was back in the early 1950s. In fact, even more urgently so. Indeed, it is now open to question whether the United Kingdom itself will survive the European experiment with Britain's half-in, half-out status. The alternative would be to suffer immense cost for no return – and no British Prime Minister could survive that politically.

Unfortunately, London's patent lack of statecraft has left Britain in an awful position both in relation to influence in the EU and power in the UN.

The need for statecraft

Thankfully, there might be reasons to believe the world is not heading back to the nineteenth century. States have been progressively socialised by international institutions and by globalisation. But much of Europe prior to 1914 was already pretty socialised, probably too socialised, so there is certainly no room for complacency. What is needed urgently is a return to effective statecraft. As crises erupt and emerge, it is the big power state that will continue to shape and shove the international system. International institutions are likely to be reduced to being either legitimisers of state action, organisers of supporting coalitions, or merely marginalised. Paradoxically, self- or auto-declining powers, those that have chosen to wane, rely on both institutions and a concept of influence therein to mask their decline. Britain for example could play a much more influential role on the world stage than it does in that fashion. But to do so would require grand strategy and statecraft allied to the sustained application of all national means to shape such an environment: via institutions, but also in its own right and with all-important state partnerships. For reasons of political culture and financial austerity the British have effectively decided they no longer wish to play a game they went a very long way to creating. With the end of the Cold War, the foreign and security apparatus of Great Britain, but also of most European states radically shifted gear. Power politics were out, international intervention was in. These days, foreign and security departments remain brim full of counter-terrorism experts and aid and development specialists, which skew national strategies towards failed states and civil strife. This keeps the late twentieth century alive by emphasising issues and strategies that have simply been overtaken and sidelined in the world of realpolitik.

The consequence is a perfect storm for the West: a retreat from the post-war values of institutionalised power born of the shock of systemic war and old power reticence about the use of raw power. Add to that the weakening of American internationalism in the wake of a decade lost in the deserts of Afghanistan and bemired in the swamps of Mesopotamia, which has eroded US financial, military and moral reserves. This is accelerating into a crisis for western-inspired liberal internationalism. The very concept of European 'power' is creating a vacuum, which is being occupied by the likes of China and to some extent Russia (although the latter suffers from huge contradictions of its own).[5] The prestige of the West upon which both the UN and EU were founded is in the process of being fatally damaged and weakened, primarily by the negligence of the West's own leaders and the inability of European leaders in particular to adapt to new realities.

The UN and EU share certain characteristics. Both were conceived as attempts to prevent extreme state behaviour, one at the global level, the other at the European level. However, the proto-internationalism of the 1950s and 1960s failed to ever come close to converting the leading state powers to a Kantian notion of world or universal government, however imperfect. Both the UN and the EU now struggle to constrain state power. Even as they profess their love for both institutions, Germany is eclipsing the EU, whilst China, the US and other G20 states eclipse the UN. In effect, their moment has passed; their only real hope was to switch from being an antidote to the presumed poisons of nation state power to being more efficient aggregators of state power.

Where both the UN and EU have helped to prevent extreme state behaviour it has been mainly that of weak states. To some extent, these institutions provided a platform of legitimacy for state action to constrain the more dangerous resources now available for state influence – such as nuclear weapons. The impending Iran nuclear crisis could well mark the swan song of such efforts. Locked in a potentially deadly tango with the West over its efforts to acquire nuclear weapons, Iran is upping the ante in response to threats of Western sanctions. Provocations range from test-firing medium-range surface-to-air missiles to naval exercises in the Straits of Hormuz to intimidate the Gulf States and show the world that it could close the most important oil shipping lane in the event of a future confrontation with the United States and its European allies.

The critical legitimacy the UN and EU conferred has been progressively undermined over many years. The reasons are manifold. The UN and the EU have themselves fallen into disrepute, their reputations marred by intransparency of process, misappropriation of funds, and last but not least incapacity to provide workable solutions to pressing problems. Globalisation has led to the progressive marketisation of world politics, shifting power from the states to the market. Technological advances and technology spread has weakened the control regimes can exercise. Add to this a crisis of popular and political legitimacy and the institutions in New York and Brussels appear in the eyes of many (particularly of those who are net budget contributors) as at best otherworldly and irrelevant, at worst corrupt.

Solidarity, fairness and the emergence of market power

As has already been said, both the UN and EU were mechanisms designed to transfer resources from the rich north and west to the poor south and east – in Europe and the wider world. That worked in the ideological climate of the Cold War and when memberships were relatively small. However, the UN has today grown to 192 members compared with 51 in 1945 and the EU to 27 member-states compared with 6 in 1951.[6] Nowadays, state leaderships are legitimised either by democracy or growth or a mix of the two. Indeed, people still look to the state rather than institutions for essential public goods, something reinforced by the emergence of Asian power. In those many places where the post-colonial state has failed and with it the brave new worlds of enlargement and development, Western taxpayers are refusing to fund aid via institutions such as the UN and EU, which they mistrust. Instead, they prefer to use non-governmental conduits or simply not to pay at all.

Ultimately, it is the failure of both institutions to properly oversee and uphold the rules-based international system for which they were created which is leading to their marginalisation. Too often both the UN and EU have tolerated those in treaty-breach or favoured a few at the expense of the many. This is particularly the case for the EU where the whole Eurozone crisis has been triggered by the rogue behavior of the primary architects of the single currency. It was after all France and Germany, who first cavalierly flouted the very rules of the Stability and Growth Pact they had established by bursting through enshrined budget deficit and public debt ceilings.[7] Paris and Berlin routinely interpret 'Europe' as to mean the defence of their own vital and essential interest. But no institution can survive the perennial absence of solidarity and fairness.

There are other drivers of change that challenge both an institutions-based system and state-centric power. Technology has seen the breakdown of formal diplomacy. Leaders and peoples talk to each other, as the Third Parties of international politics are increasingly bypassed. The global reach of deregulated financial markets means that state power is increasingly subject to market power. This is particularly true for those states desperate to access loans with a reasonable rate of interest. Be it the role of bond markets in the Eurozone crisis or the fall-out from the impending European banking collapse, it is not difficult to grasp how much systemic power is now subject to the 'rules' of the market. The very essence of economic globalisation is the destruction of regulation. International institutions have failed to effectively shape, let alone combat this new systemic anarchy.

State power without apologies

Perhaps the most telling sign of power shift away from the West and its institutions has been the emergence of Asian power, incarnated most prominently by the reach of its sovereign wealth. Beijing announced on 27 December, 2011 that the China National Petroleum Corporation (CNPC) would begin looking for oil in

Afghanistan's Amu Darya Basin, which is estimated to hold around 87 million barrels of oil. As the West prepares to leave Afghanistan having spent huge amounts of treasure and at the cost of many lives, China and the other neighbours are preparing to exploit Afghanistan's $1 trillion of mineral reserves. Much of the first half of the new century will be spent trying to cope with China's rapacious appetite for natural resources. Indeed, only sustained economic growth will offset the marked absence of political liberty in China. China's move into Afghanistan also marks another step on the road to a new bipolar world dominated by Beijing and Washington.

On 26 December economists at the Centre for Economics and Business Research (CEBR) announced that Brazil had overtaken Britain as the world's sixth largest economy.[8] They also predicted that India and Russia would enjoy surges in growth as the old West stagflates into what the CEBR has called Europe's 'lost next decade'. The only consolation for the British was that the CEBR confidently predicted that by 2020 Britain would have a significantly larger economy than that of France. Whether Brazil manages to turn such paper wealth into power remains to be seen, but Britain and France really do now need to decide the extent of their strategic ambitions.

Sadly, the West seems incapable of thinking big enough to cope with this new reality, particularly the European West. The Eurozone crisis is of such severity that, rather like heroin addicts, many European leaders will sell their peoples' futures for a short-term political fix, rather than deal with the real problem. As Luxembourg Prime Minister Jean-Claude Juncker put it over Christmas 2011, 'We know how to solve the problem, we just do not know how to get re-elected afterwards'.[9] Europe only recognises as much strategy as it can afford . . . which is not a lot.

The immediate challenges for the UN and the EU

In the immediate future the essential challenge for the UN will be the structure and membership of the UN Security Council and its relationship in turn with the General Assembly. The UN Security Council was designed to be a security mechanism, hence its name. If the UN Security Council (UNSC) is to retain its mission to ensure compliance with the UN Charter, particularly the security chapters, then the criteria for power for permanent membership must be military power. Today, the world's top five military powers in terms of capability and experience are the US, UK, France, Russia and China – in that order.[10] So, the existing members should be maintained.

However, many of the emerging and not-so-emerging powers see the UN Security Council as a kind of World Board or UN Executive Committee for which they demand other criteria to be established as the basis for permanent membership – economic power (Germany), population (Brazil, India, Indonesia et al). However, such a change in the mandate and structure of the UN Security Council would also change the function of the UNSC and its relationship with the UN General Assembly, as it would have to deal with a host of issues other than the security chapters of the UN Charter.

This in turn would raise particular issues as to where best to conduct crisis management at the UN, and the relationship with sub-contracting institutions such as the EU, the Organisation for Security and Co-operation in Europe and NATO. Such a shift would also raise issues over the Secretary-General's mandate and role in crises, in particular the control of UN operations via the Department for Peacekeeping Operations. The need for reform is pressing, as evinced by the relatively weak command and control and thus performance of UN agencies in UN-mandated missions such as Afghanistan. This issue will become increasingly pressing if the North American and Western European taxpayer are expected to continue to foot much of the bill. Indeed, the issue of taxation and representation will be central to all efforts to reform both the UN and EU.

The EU is once more facing the very dilemma it was created to resolve – the German question. The EU and its precursors were first and foremost designed to constrain Germany. Implicit since then has been an essential balance of power at the heart of the Union, with

German economic power offset by British and French economic and military power. This has confirmed the role and utility of Britain in Europe but has offered the British nothing in return. With the downgrading of France's AAA status by credit-rating agency Standard & Poor's, the marginalisation of Britain within the EU and the export-led growth afforded Germany by the Eurozone/customs union, such a balance no longer exists.

Paradoxically, south and east Europe want more of the Union because they have little faith in their own governments. A less charitable explanation for their federalist zeal would be of course that they are net recipients rather than contributors. In essence, the Eurozone crisis demonstrates the extent to which south and east Europe has become addicted to west and north European money. However, the west and north European taxpayer is no longer willing to pay for the flawed experiment that is the EU. If the EU fails there is every chance of dangerous instability on Europe's periphery.

What will likely come out of the Eurozone crisis is a 'special relationship' between Germany and the European Commission, with the European Council reduced to being a weak senate. The already dangerous democratic deficit of the European construction could then become critical because the European Parliament is neither up to the task of effective political oversight, nor is it trusted by the people of Europe to undertake such a role.

There will be many euphemisms to hide German power. But the essential fact is that Germany has assumed the leadership of the Eurozone in the current crisis, and the Union is already showing signs of becoming an Imperium. Others might be forced to accept German leadership, but Britain never will. Unless a new strategic partnership between London and Berlin is achieved, the British could go off to join an 'Anglosphere'. That would mark the beginning of the end for the EU as the implicit balance of power upon which it was established would unmistakably fail.

Looking ahead

The twenty-first century will be hyper-competitive and state-centric with security posing globalised rather than regionalised challenges. Given rapid changes in economy, demography, technology and capability, the power stakes for states will be very high indeed. Two essential dynamics will drive conflict. First, states will compete and sometimes dangerously. Second, with the failure of states ever smaller, more extreme groups are likely to get their hands on ever more dangerous resources. In the absence of new intellectual and institutional underpinnings for co-operation, coming competition could well become increasingly informal and unpredictable. Driven on by new factors such as the global financial markets and their propensity for cliff-edge speculation with state debt, such wrestling could eventually prove dangerous. State influence will once again become the global currency with any pretense to global altruism much reduced. Indeed, as Asia emerges the principles of Western liberal internationalism as represented in the UN and EU will erode. Therefore, hanging on to outmoded institutions at all costs could well become the strategic equivalent of putting the institutional cart before the strategic horse.

States will have to face up to the consequences of profound change. However, recent crises have revealed elites in Europe's power states dangerously resistant to such political courage. For the EU, either a new 'trirectoire' will emerge between Germany, Britain and France or new/old groupings will form such as the Anglosphere, which would lead to the breaking up of the EU. Much of the future direction and stability of Europe will depend on Germany and the sensitivity and quality of German leadership, irrespective of and independent to the EU and its proliferating agencies.

For the UN to survive as a credible security institution, there will need to be a genuine and shared strategic concept. This would require the great powers that now comprise the G20 to agree and coalesce around the why, the where, the when and the how of collective security action. Even the briefest analysis of past informal regimes suggest that this will be unlikely. However, absent such a strategic concept the UN will be doomed more than ever to death by a thousand meetings, a talking shop for the aggrieved, the small and the powerless. Spheres of influence and balances of power have already returned as states such as China and Russia reject the notion that Western created institutions could constrain their power.

The way forward? For the leading European powers, only a return to statecraft offers any real hope of credible and effective influence in the twenty-first century. That will mean the formal and clear enunciation of reasoned and reasonable goals upon which to construct political coalitions, the legitimisation of those goals, the formalisation of diplomacy and process, the crafting of criteria for action that are adhered to, and the building of a popular coalition through effective strategic communications. The UN and EU will never die but, like old soldiers they might simply fade away.

Notes

1 See Prado C. G., *Descartes and Foucault: A Contrastive Introduction to Philosophy* (1992; Ottawa: University of Ottawa Press), p.143.

2 On 11 May 1953 in the House of Commons, Winston Churchill attacked France for its 'anti-British position'. See Lindley-French, J., *A Chronology of European Security and Defence: 1945–2007* (2007; Oxford: Oxford University Press), p. 43.

3 In 1651 Thomas Hobbes wrote in *Leviathan*, 'For by Art is created that great LEVIATHAN called a COMMON-WEALTH or STATE, which is but an ARTIFICIAL MAN, though of greater stature and strength than the Natural,

whose protection and defence it was intended.' See Tuck,
R. (ed.), *Hobbes, Leviathan* (1991; Cambridge: Cambridge
University Press) p.9.

4 The consequence of the British 'fudge' over the EU can be
seen today in the current British Government's convoluted
argument. London claims that it will seek to re-negotiate
Britain's membership if there is deeper European integration
to preserve the Euro. The entire logic of deeper integration is that no such space will in future exist for Britain to
occupy. As Samuel Brittan wrote in the *Financial Times* on
27 September 2012, 'Although there was always a strong
federalist element in the background, the post-1945 European
movement began in earnest with the Schuman Plan, designed
to integrate German and French coal and steel industries so
that war between the two countries would be impossible.
There followed the common market, designed to free up
trade in western Europe; and I can remember urging Harold
Macmillan, the British prime minister, to get on with his application to join. But as time went on, the EU, as it became,
acquired more and more ambitions and a whole cadre of Eurocrats developed, concerned with increasing EU power and
influence for its own sake. At this point they lost me. In recent
economic policy it has achieved the worst of both worlds.
It has constructed a network of regulation and red tape, of
which business rightly complains. But it has combined this
with highly restrictive macroeconomic policies, suggesting
that the Bourbons in charge have learnt nothing and forgotten
nothing from the catastrophic experiences of the 1930s.'

5 In a sense much of Europe has abandoned the use of hard
power as being in any way legitimate. This is apparent in
much of the language of the EU's Common Foreign and
Security Policy and its emphasis on so-called 'effective
multilateralism'. The paradox is that in an attempt to accommodate Germany and its angst over power, Europe is likely to
become less militarily powerful just when Germany is on the
ascent within Europe. Post-modern Europe will have to face
the decidedly modern rest of the world.

6 See www.un.org/membership.
7 To underpin the Euro, the original Maastricht Convergence Criteria set as irreducible benchmarks government deficit at no higher than 3%, whilst government debt could be no higher than 60%. From 1997 on France and Germany repeatedly argued that this was too 'inflexible'. By 2005 the European Commission said that French and German infractions had weakened the criteria. Interestingly, neither Berlin nor Paris were ever sanctioned whereas Portugal (2002) and Greece (2005) were. There was clearly one rule for the powerful and another for the weak.
8 According to the CEBR press release, not only did Brazil overtake the UK, but by 2020 the Russian economy would be the fourth biggest and India would be the fifth biggest. However, the UK would overtake France in 2016. See www.cebr.com/wp-content/uploads/cebr-World-Economic-League-Tables-press-release-26-December-2011.pdf
9 See *The Economist* blog of 3 May 2012, 'The Eurozone Crisis: Call it a Depression'; www.economist.com/blogs/2012/eurozone crisis.
10 See IISS, *The Military Balance* (2012; Oxford: Oxford University Press).

– 10: The Euro – Uniformity and Diversity –

T owards the end of this century, historians may well look back and wonder just how our generation could have overlooked the glaringly obvious design flaws of the common currency, the euro. Perusing the records of various national and European institutions, they will find it astonishing that vital differences between countries invited to form the Eurozone had been utterly disregarded. How could knowledgeable leaders have believed that all of a sudden the Greeks would behave like the Germans and the Spanish become Dutch? We, who live now and will have mostly disappeared by then, know the answer. We are the living witnesses, or the children and grandchildren of those who partook and suffered in the cataclysms of the great continental wars of the twentieth century. Therefore we understand quite well the huge political drive to unite the European continent and eliminate any conceivable source of conflict between its states; and we know that the 'euro project' was consciously designed as a primarily political project although presented as an economic one. We also know that the historical lesson of playing politics with currencies is fatally flawed. They bite back. Yet in order to save Europe from social and political disintegration, or from the fascist politics that the European 'project' was supposed to banish forever, we have to think now about the conundrum that is the euro.

It has been an enchanting idea for us, the varied people of this hugely complex continent: living together as one enormous family, sharing our wealth without bloody encounters. The trouble is that the principal members of this family, like those of many another families, are not readily compatible. In the routine of our daily lives, we are now in the habit of crossing national boundaries within the European continent with remarkable ease. We might still occasionally have to display our passports but they are rarely accorded more than a courtesy glance by the relevant authorities. Sunning ourselves on a Spanish beach, eating a light lunch in an Italian villa or traversing the Rhine valley in a German train, we barely notice that we are abroad. This is exactly how it should be within the confines of a family, in the broadest sense of that term. This is why we find it so hard to understand, to appreciate and to absorb the massive economic and financial differences between the south and the north of the same continent. How can our uncles and aunts, siblings and cousins, have such divergent attitudes when it comes to the basics of life?

The creation of the European common currency followed the opposite trajectory to most currency creations in human history. Currencies tend to come into being once there is already a viable and well established political entity to provide their foundation. English sterling achieved international status long after it had a state and a national bank to give it justification and meaning. The same applies to the French franc, the Austrian schilling, the Dutch guilder, the German mark, the US dollar and most other forms of money that have ever been usefully employed in international markets. In recognition of this fact, and to give a useful barter value to the money, a facsimile of the ruling monarch (or in the absence of a monarch, some other meaningful symbol) was affixed to one side of the coin or note guaranteeing its worth. In addition, all traders using a currency to transact their commerce could rest assured knowing precisely how much gold or silver was at stake in relation to the traded items. In other words, there were no doubts regarding the value of the money that was the cornerstone of each and every deal.

Even as late as the fourth quarter of the last century the remnants of the crucial bond between the noble metal and the various manifestations of currency still survived. But today the real value of currencies barely depends on the quantity of gold held safely in the depths of central bank cellars. In the British case, it was a conscious decision by Mr Gordon Brown, early on in the Blair Government, to sell almost all the British Gold Reserves as a contribution towards the so-called 'demonetisation' of gold. It was a vain effort; but Mr Brown did manage to choose the very lowest point in recent decades in the price of gold to deprive his country of this ancient and enduring measure of value. (It is not without relevance that gold is cherished not only for its scarcity but also for its independence from political control.)

As the business of determining the exact value of any currency has never been very straightforward, the market has shrewdly considered the wealth and productivity of a country as the guarantor of its money. Each currency thus largely rests on the economic substance of a particular state. This still is the case for the US dollar, the British pound, the Chinese yuan or the Russian rouble. The trouble with the euro, and one the principal sources of the current malaise is the simple asymmetry between an existent currency and a non-existent state with a corresponding economy at its base.

The single currency has shackled together vastly differing countries and economies. The persisting travails of Greece, Portugal, Spain and Italy are in a spectacular contrast with the case of Holland, Finland, Estonia, Austria and above all, of course, Germany. The first group is substantially over-borrowed while their northern counterparts appear relatively stable and balanced. The market is well aware of this distinction and the price of bonds reflects quite accurately the situation of each country. Thus Spain and Italy pay an unsustainable interest rate of nearly 7% on their borrowings, whereas Germany pays just over 1%. Put simply, the present and dangerous crisis manifests itself in the inability of the countries of southern Europe to repay their debt within a reasonable time-frame.

While Rome burns, figuratively speaking (if not literally, as yet), we are busy drowning in a sea of words. Professionals in the field of economics and finance are searching the past trying to forecast various possible futures. Politicians are busy attending endlessly inconclusive meetings, to emerge with solutions, which may or more probably may not work. Unable to grasp what actually has happened, or how to remedy this untenable situation, we must surely start with the obvious question: why did we create the euro in the first place? What was the matter with the seventeen currencies that the euro replaced? The Dutch guilder, the German mark, as well as other 'northern' European currencies, were all in reasonable shape, and none were in need of replacement. In contrast, the financial situation of the southern European countries – Portugal, Greece, Spain and Italy – was somewhat parlous at the moment of conversion to the euro. As is now well known, Goldman Sachs were paid to help the Greeks cook their books so that they too could fulfill the entry criteria. But it was not their fault alone: the creators of the euro connived.[1] The conversion of these currencies was something of a godsend. The countries concerned were given a currency which was stable and which no longer required revaluation every five years or so. The causal relationship between the economies of these countries and their indigenous currency was broken, and replaced by the less gaugeable European economy and its transnational currency.

The impulse for the replacement of national monies could not have been justified on economic or financial grounds. In reality, a common currency had long been a major ambition of proponents of a unified European state, well before the Maastricht Treaty of 1992. The creation of such a state, envisaged between two world wars by Jean Monnet, Robert Schuman and others, was not to be accomplished in one generation. The federalists have always been patient, dogged and determined. From the beginning of the long drawn-out saga of the European project, they have been skillful at using every crisis to move one step closer to the creation of a single European state. With the euro, these political forces stumbled upon a win-win strategy, as the new coin held hope on both of its sides. On one side the promise (albeit unlikely) that that the weaker economies would somehow catch up with their stronger counterparts in the north. Unlikely, because you cannot alter the economy of a country and the centuries-old habits of its people by simply changing its currency. This obvious fact never bothered the creators of the euro because they considered the other side of the new coin, the possibility of it provoking a crisis triggering more integration as even more valuable. As a matter of fact, believers in an ever-closer union have anticipated the divergence of underlying economic fundamentals and the resulting crisis we are experiencing today. This is no wild imagining: they say as much when they are asked. Their term for such a state of affairs is 'creative crisis', because in such times it is possible to jump people into decisions to which they would not otherwise agree. As the federalists are fond of saying, the result of every crisis in the last sixty years has been 'more Europe'. And they are not wrong. The current situation is indeed severe enough to require for its final resolution both banking union, fiscal union and economic union: in short, the creation of a single European economy. And this uniform single economy is the principal pre-condition for the creation of their long-desired, unified European state.

Thus the origin of the euro, its *raison d'être*, and the political forces assembled behind the creation of this artificially conceived currency, are clear enough. Beyond looking at its emergence and its progenitors, the next question to address is the position of the euro in the financial world of today.

As I have said, the way in which currencies were evaluated historically was to relate them to the economy of their guarantor state. The financial markets judged the drachma in relation to the Greek economy, the deutschmark in relation to the German economy, pound sterling in relation to the British economy, and so on. The value of the euro, similarly, ought to be tied to the economy of a single state. But here is the rub: the euro is not a function of any individual state economy.

It is one of a kind, a creature never seen or experienced hitherto.

At the most superficial level, the present crisis is about government debt. The southern countries of Europe are incapable of repaying their debts in a timely and orderly fashion, if at all. As a result, the financial markets are only providing further loans to help out these countries with an interest rate of not less than six per cent. But borrowing at above six per cent, the Greeks would in very short order go bankrupt. Meanwhile, the solvency of Portugal is in doubt, while the Spanish and the Italians are finding it increasingly difficult to borrow the requisite amounts of money. These threats are even clouding the French horizon. Belatedly waking up to economic reality, two of the major three credit agencies demoted the safety level of the country's credit rating in the first half of 2012, from a comfortable AAA to AA+ and Aaa, respectively. An American agency, Egan-Jones Ratings, has gone so far as to downgrade French debt to a humiliating and anxious BBB+.

In the run-up to the financial crisis, a few discerning voices highlighted the precipitate decline of asset prices in the financial markets world-wide. These observers noted the volatile and unpredictable character of the market, its hysterical response to a world seemingly swirling out of control. Hence, they concluded that the market could not give any firm indication of the financial state or economic condition of individual countries, let alone of the world economy. According to this line of reasoning, the vast majority of economists (within and outside of government), the banks and the commercial world, had generally misjudged the situation and thereby contributed to the current crisis.

To blame 'the market' in the present crisis has the priceless advantage of being answerless: there is no one to say 'I am the market and what you say about me is profoundly misconceived.' The 'market', huge and complex as it is, lives and functions as markets have always done and will do for the rest of time. You bring your cow to market with the intention of selling it for the best price attainable. Whoever wishes to buy it will try to pay you as little as possible. You will argue, bargain and come to a deal. Of course, the final price may be influenced by how many other cows are around and how many people want a cow that day. The seller and buyer will probably pay a little for using the facilities. But the market itself will remain absolutely neutral. It has nothing to contribute to the debate.

In their critical stance towards the market, these no doubt talented analysts fall prey to one general and critical misconception. The 'market', in the common parlance of today, refers to a few financial centres – New York, London, Beijing and Hong-Kong, among others – where currencies, shares, bonds, and basic commodities are traded unceasingly. These centres are so vast, so diverse and complex that no single human intelligence can be said to control them. When trading professionals, embroiled in the minutiae of daily deals, refer to the 'market' they usually refer to a minor and secluded section of it. The market simply varies too much in its substances and locations to accommodate any intelligent general point of reference.

At this difficult economic moment it is more crucial than ever to understand the true functioning of the market. The simplest way of understanding its role is to think of it as a football referee. The referee's whistle and the market transaction are equally final. Except that our referee is in deep trouble in two respects: the complexity and the wide range of the market make a single overview of the pitch almost impossible. In addition, the massive financial interference by governments distorts the picture. As if our referee has to officiate several matches simultaneously. And to make matters worse, the availability of virtually unlimited sums of money will inevitably influence the outcome of matches to come.

The intricacies of the market create a new kind of fear in the minds of analysts and leading political decision-makers. Seen in this light, the current posturing of political and economic actors is not about how to make the economies of the southern European states competitive. It is about trying to change the perception of the market in order to raise enough money, in enough time, to deal with economically fragile actualities. If this money is not found, somehow and from somewhere, the world's entire financial edifice may crumble, or so we are told.

We live in a strange universe. Greece represents less than 2 per cent of the EU's economy and it cannot represent more than a fraction of 1 per cent of the planet's financial well-being. If its present troubles can be accused of causing such an overwhelming collapse, we are indeed in a world that hangs by the thinnest of threads. I do not believe that any scenario involving a Greek financial collapse corresponds to such a reality. Very few rational beings think otherwise. How is it possible, then, for such hysteria to infect the thinking of our most responsible politicians?

In part this can be explained by the complexity and wide-ranging extensions of the market, which have created a new kind of fear in the minds of analysts and political decision makers. And, in turn, the correspondingly heavy hand of governmental intervention inevitably distorts the daily workings of the market. Under these conditions, a leap of faith is required when we turn our attention to the future. At the same time, we do know more or less where we stand. The euro, created with a promise of bringing all its participant states to much closer economic and financial parity, has achieved precisely the opposite. The gap between the north and the south is so vast that keeping them together in one currency is by now a pipe dream. So what about the future? Where do we go from here? What options do we really have? Let us evaluate them one at a time.

The first possibility is to continue as before, saving

the ailing south with a massive cash-injection from the north. The form and the amount of such transfers is the stuff of every EU conference these days. Is austerity or economic stimulus the way to go? How much money is sufficient? Exactly which country should provide it, how and when are these loans expected to be repaid? What are the obligations of the creditor nations and what are those of the debtors? Is the emerging financial architecture – with a 'creatively' operating European Central Bank and rescue fund – still compatible with existing EU and national laws? These questions are far from easy to answer. But while discussion rages, the continuing build-up of pressure means that the break up of the Euro seems only a matter of time. With the imminent demise of Greece, and the clear and present danger to Portugal, Spain and Italy, the euro is unable to survive in its present form beyond two or three years. But a dramatic end-game may come even sooner than anticipated.

If the south and the north cannot be held together, the second option would be to let each country within the Eurozone revert to its own currency. Changing the currency of a state is not an easy matter. When the euro was created, eleven countries decided at the outset to adopt it. To the great surprise of many observers, the transition was easier than expected. Everything was well organised and there were remarkably few instances of serious frustration either for individuals or for banks. According to the same logic, there is no reason to believe that engineering the reverse should be any different. But there is one crucial difference between moving from drachma or lira to the euro and reverting back to drachma and lira from the common currency. It is the difference between moving from the sunlight to darkness and then returning from darkness to broad daylight. Living in flattering obscurity allowed – it even encouraged – southerners to become oblivious to the true value of their economy. Hauling them back into the sunshine will force them to experience reality again, with currency values determined by actual economic activity.

This is precisely what most average politicians fear, and what only outstanding statesmen (who are few and far between) have the courage to advocate. The difference is obvious: it is easy to ride the prevailing tide; it is infinitely harder to turn the tide around. Churchill and Roosevelt, de Gaulle and Hitler come to mind when thinking of the giants who radically changed the public mood instead of drifting with the flow. As no such leader is visible on the horizon – particularly not in Germany or France – we can safely dismiss this second option. The disintegration of the common currency, left to its diminishing resources, may take a few more convulsive years and a few more crises. But there can no longer be any doubt that the euro, in its present form, is doomed. No currency can possibly survive which tries to serve a number of radically divergent economies. This is a truth recognised even by the pro-European integrationist political forces. Which is precisely why they are desperate to use the common currency to force incompatible economies into a straight line. Their obstacle is that while a common economy may succeed in giving birth to a unified currency – as happened in the United States sixty years after its creation – an artificially unified currency can never, on its own, create a common economy.

So is there a third alternative, other than sudden, complete disintegration or more gradual but equally terminal decline? Possibly so, were we to act on the belief that every healthy currency has to reflect the economy at its base. Southerners, as well as northerners, each have economies similar enough to sustain a single common currency. The economic profiles of the Mediterranean belt of Greece, Portugal, Spain and Italy are close enough to partake in a second-order, weaker euro. Such a euro might well be subject to the same periodic revaluations as these countries' currencies have always historically enjoyed. Let us call this currency euro No. 2 or, perhaps, 'eurosud'? Similarly, the northern economies of Germany, Austria, Holland, Finland, Estonia and the Czech Republic are sufficiently close to each other to provide the common ground for a separate currency. Let us call this the euro No. 1 or, perhaps, 'euronord'? The division of the euro into two distinct entities would be less traumatic than its sudden or gradual disintegration. More importantly, the relation of these two currencies to their diverse and yet

compatible underlying economic realities would give
them true substance and help them to survive in an
ever more complex financial world.

So now we come to the elephant in the room. What
about France? How does she fit into a thus divided
Europe? The short answer to these questions is simple:
France does not naturally fit into either the southern or
the northern side of the equation. But there is nothing
new here, for the peculiar situation of France in Europe has been the same for almost two hundred years.
Since the era of Napoleonic glory, France has lost the
ability to maintain her prime position on the continent by relying on her strength alone. The definitive
French defeat by an emerging Germany in 1871, in the
Franco-Prussian War, set the pattern. And although the
world could clearly see the Bismarck-inspired transformation of the continent and the fundamental erosion
of French hegemony, the political ramifications of this
transformation took a century to unfold.

Thus do we come to the belle époque and the one
event which set the stage imperceptibly for what was
to happen to Europe over the next one hundred years.
The Entente Cordiale, brain-child of French foreign
minister Théophile Delcassé and signed by France
and Great Britain in 1904, has never been accorded
by historians the monumental status that it deserves.
And yet this one agreement set the scene of world politics for a century. If Britain and France had not been
allies, the First World War would have been a brief

local conflagration raising Germany to the pinnacle of Europe. If no First World War, then no emergence of Hitler and certainly no Second World War. If no Second World War, we would not have a European Union in its current form. If no EU, then no euro. If no euro, probably, no crisis, certainly no crisis of the current dimensions. We would have had German hegemony for a century and be quite used to it by now instead of being faced with it in new clothes, via the euro crisis.

Arthur James Balfour, who negotiated the Entente Cordiale agreement on behalf of the British side, is the great-uncle of my wife. He achieved a great deal both in politics and beyond. He has been one of the key figures in the creation of Israel and his famous declaration is an almost unique example of a document that so vastly changed world history. So I have to say with a heavy heart that the consequences of the Entente Cordiale were, simply and massively, tragic. Even today, when considering the intrinsic difficulties of the position of France, we have to hark back to the unfortunate Entente as the original, and sinful, cause.

So what are the options for France, given the north/south division? To be part of the north, she would have to accept the undisputed leadership of Germany. To be pre-eminent within the south she would have to accept operating on a lower economic level. Neither choice is attractive to her political class, which has long been in the habit of living at the top. But economic and financial realities cannot be forever denied. In the end, they will still determine the final configuration of any continent. Fortunately the upper tiers of French political life are trained to function even in the most challenging environment. It would be no surprise to see a France of considerable power and influence survive in either of the two segments. Whatever is achieved will be due to her exclusive and exceptional political class. So what will the French elite choose to do? Upon that choice much else depends.

Note

1 http://www.spiegel.de/international/europe/greek-debt-crisis-how-goldman-sachs-helped-greece-to-mask-its-true-debt-a-676634.html

Johanna Möhring

– The Destiny of the Nation State –

> History teaches us that men and nations behave wisely
> once they have exhausted all other alternatives.
> – Abba Eban, 16 December 1970

S o why has the nation state been so conspicuously absent from political discourse and academic research for the last twenty years? Michael Lind, writing in this volume, pointed out that the dream of a world society uniting all human beings in brotherly bonds is an idea that reappears cyclically. Throughout the ages, like a wandering comet, it appears in the political skies after cataclysmic events. Thus in the twentieth century, the catastrophes of the First and Second World Wars had provided the intellectual and emotional boost to launch institutional integration of Western Europe from above. Deep in the dark valley of the 1930s and 40s, even dyed in the wool classical liberals reneged on their cherished principles of individual political and economic freedom.[1] Supranational authority – a solidarity union among western democracies – appeared as the only thinkable political alternative to national-socialist and communist totalitarianism.

Each of these cycles of cosmopolitan experiment

seems to last about one human lifetime. Shamed, chastened and mortified, after an episode like the smashing of the Third Reich, there is an understandable and human attraction in setting out – once again – to pursue 'a remote and ideal object, which captivates the imagination by its splendour and the reason by its simplicity',[2] as Lord Acton put it. The unexpected and unpredicted end of the Cold War, whose numerous proxy wars consumed millions in lives and billions in treasure triggered the latest infatuation with cosmopolitanism.

Compared to the first half of the twentieth century we live in happier times. This allows us to contemplate the current state of affairs in a calm if not leisurely fashion. Clearly, the nation state has not been relegated to the dustbin of history. On the contrary, as Michael Gove wrote in his preface, allegiance to nation states still throbs in people's hearts, an assessment echoed by most authors throughout this collection. No other frame of reference currently exists to organise public life in a sufficiently democratic fashion. And the deficiencies of multilateral governance in general, and the current travails of the European Union in particular, tell us not to hold our breath.

Pierre Manent, a liberal French thinker (and therefore a rare creature among the phalanx of overwhelmingly left-wing French intellectuals) describes the European condition poetically: throughout the ages, Europeans have excelled at inventing daring political edifices, 'thrown like arcs across the ravines of time.'[3]

Every time ossification has threatened, Europeans have managed to come up with something new. Thus, two of the greatest political and cultural inventions came into being, the sovereign state and representative government. Fused as the 'nation state', they have allowed countless people to enjoy the fruits of civilisation and of liberty.

Perhaps it is time to invent something new yet again? The post-modern cosmopolitan narrative is clearly in crisis, with international and supranational institutions failing to provide answers to the world's and Europe's pressing problems. But is the nation state faring much better? After all, it appears weakened, struggling to provide security and safety in an uncertain world. Is it not buckling under the strains of economic and financial crisis, unable to call global market forces to heel? Superficially, its social fabric seems to be un-ravelling, weakened by consumerist disinterest and by religious and cultural affirmations of non-participating minorities. Affiliation with, let alone active participation in the political process is dwindling. So given its current travails, might not the nation state have run its course as well?

The blunt answer to this question is that the nation state is all we have left standing. Philip Bobbitt has theorised the imminent replacement of the nation state by the 'market state', responsible for maximising opportunity of each individual citizen.[4] Were this true, the nation state would indeed lose its leading role in defining political choices and loyalties. But the present moment of economic and financial turmoil suggests that Bobbitt's vision of the market state will not come to pass. People look to the nation state for answers. We do not fight alone, nor, more prosaically, do we save alone. Sacrifices can only be asked on behalf of a collective for which people feel enduring affection and loyalty. To denigrate such feelings, to deny them, or worse, to scorn them as 'jingoistic' or 'nationalist', is a grave error of political judgment. Because we can be certain of only a few things. Nations do exist. Trying to stamp out national feelings for the sake of some higher goal is bound to fail. Hugh Seton-Watson, an English historian keenly interested in nationalist movements and state formation especially in the seething cauldron of the Balkans, pithily observed that to do so will merely 'increase the sum total of explosive human hatred in the world'.[5]

For cultural reasons, developed over centuries, nations, and national characteristics with them, have proved resistant to change. Much as proponents of globalisation and European unification might wish otherwise, the exchange of goods, services and information, migration and instant communication have not eroded them. Yes, the spread of global brands has brought a certain uniform look to the shopping precincts of our cities. But look more closely, and each internationally operating firm is subtly catering to local tastes, adapting its message to suit a specific national context. Neither has the communication revolution brought nations truly closer together. In order to exchange more than superficial pleasantries, there first needs to be a willingness to engage in a conversation. That simple lesson is especially true for the manifestly disunited 'European Union' (EU). Low-cost airlines might be ferrying stag parties to Mallorca or Tallinn at the drop of a hat; European students might be spending a sybaritic semester or two abroad at public expense in the EU's 'Erasmus' programme, but familiarity is not the same as unity.

Despite being armed with powerful microscopes and binoculars, Brussels bureaucrats have so far been unable to detect even the slightest manifestation of a European 'demos'. Opinion polls all march doggedly the other way. People are proud to be part of Europe. But such affection is intuitively expressed in national terms. Witness the surprise win of the European golf team at the Ryder Cup in September 2012. When it was time to celebrate, again, out came the national flags! And this is true for the rest of the world. As this book has explored, national feelings, which are deeply enough rooted to be called patriotic, persist, to the dismay of those who would like to look at the world through cosmopolitan-tinted post-modern spectacles.

So it seems that nations and the states that house them are with us, for the foreseeable future. Given that the nation state is currently facing strong headwinds, how is it faring at this moment in history? Is it fit for the world of the twenty-first century, where nineteenth century power politics seem to be once again on the rise? Michael Ignatieff and others have argued throughout this volume that to persist, the nation state must fulfil several basic functions. Axiomatically, it gives a nation (or several) a physical incarnation in a state, granting it sovereign autonomy. The nation state creates a democratic space, where political action is held democratically accountable. It allows a people, however diverse, to live together under one roof. As Michael Gove pointed out, it alone allows political disagreements without bloodshed. In short, it alone provides psychological as well as physical security that is visceral – literally – felt in the gut.

But even so, the nation state is not an unalloyed public good. The constantly contested question is how much should the state be involved in the life of its citizens? At one end of the spectrum is the model of the minimal, night-watchman state, responsible solely for the deterrence or defeat of external enemies, the protection of property and defence of individual freedom: a necessary evil. At the other end, the post-war welfare state is more interventionist: the state as altruism incarnate. Regardless of what individual societies might expect from their state, and the answers to that question ought to vary widely given existing cultural and historic differences, the nation state as an institution faces a set of common challenges. They can be grouped around its twin features, representative government and sovereignty.

Challenges to representative government

Daniel Hannan thinks that the vital bond between '*kratos*' (power) and '*demos*' (people) is weakening in many countries. Citizens feel more and more alienated from their political class. Mass parties are fading everywhere, with party membership dropping swiftly. For the average voter, the political process is just what the word says, a process, almost devoid of meaning. Hannan is firmly of the view that the divorce between the political class and the electorate has been driven by the infatuation of the European political class across party lines with a supra-national project for which no politically legitimate mandate could be obtained from the electorate. Where previously, political life clustered around competing political projects and parties representing specific interests of identifiable groups, differences in party programmes now appear minimal. At the same time, whole segments of society, such as the young, or the destitute, feel no longer represented by the political system. They have been relegated to being social problems.

Politicians treat voters with thinly veiled disdain, as if they were children, to be shielded from the unfortunate realities of life. With revealing candour, speaking at one of the endless stream of euro emergency meetings in 2012, that latter-day Marie Antoinette, Luxembourg's Prime Minister Jean-Claude Juncker, observed with the hauteur of the ancient regime that

'We know how to solve the crisis, we just do not know how to get re-elected afterwards.' This is belittling the ability of citizens to foresee, debate and finally accept uncomfortable choices made on their behalf. It is also slowly eviscerating popular suffrage.

According to Michael Ignatieff, the nation state has the 'state monopoly of political allegiance'. Additional layers of governance, which make the political process opaque and ultimately unaccountable, are another source of frustration for citizens of EU member states. The European Union suffers not only from a democratic deficit. No 'demos', and all 'kratos', it is the epitome of the democratic deficit, and no amount of treaty or constitutional pirouettes will be able to change that. Roger Scruton puts it perfectly when he says that the EU's overwhelming defect is that it has never persuaded the people of Europe to accept it. 'Unconditional loyalties', which are based on pre-contractual relationships, are the precondition for a functioning democracy, and always take a national form in Western Europe.

What about the 'demos' in the equation of representative government? How does a country deal with divided loyalties, such as secessionist movements, or religious expression incompatible with the nation state?

Jean Bethke Elshtain thinks that very rarely does the nationality principle find a one-to-one expression in actual geographical terms. Very roughly, she suggests, one could say that a nation exists wherever there is a collective that decides to accept the rule of the majority. Yes, multinational democracies are rarely stable. But the alternative, splitting up into ever smaller pieces is not always a workable solution. It finds its limits in considerations of economic viability and physical security. In a way, statelets and starlets suffer from the same handicap: without a powerful sponsor, making it big is next to impossible. And such sponsors have an unfortunate tendency to extract special favours.

Nevertheless, if the urge to go it alone is expressed by democratic means, the logical conclusion according to Daniel Hannan would be to arrange an amicable divorce, rather than presiding over festering discontent.

The nation state can work as a tool to control *libido dominandi*, it can sublimate the lust for power and control of individual groups. Roger Scruton would echo such thoughts, as for him, nationality refers to people consciously identifying with a certain territory and the law that prevails on its soil. How can living together be organised in a multinational state? Michael Ignatieff, speaking from fruitful Canadian experience, provides pointers. Clearly, an existing democratic political culture that federates across ethnic boundaries is a very important condition. Sufficient prosperity also plays a vital role, as economic rivalries and distributional disputes tend to fuel secessionist tendencies. Above all, the state somehow has to be perceived as a neutral player delivering a level playing field that adjudicates to each party fairly in its own eyes.

When it comes to secessionist dynamics, the European Union has acted as a centripetal and not as a centrifugal force. Rather than strengthening the internal cohesion of its member states, it has provided ideological, institutional and financial incentives for sub-national autonomy and independence. Member states such as Belgium or Spain, for example, could be forgiven for feeling like a fizzy tablet slowly dissolving between regional and EU level.

As a matter of fact, perhaps the oldest nation state there is, Great Britain, also suffers from this affliction. Frank Field thinks that it finds itself in a special form of double bind. On the one hand, power has moved to Brussels in consecutive waves of European integration. On the other hand, the process of devolution has delegated powers to the constituent parts of the Great Britain – without taking into account the special place England has as its dominant part. 'England' and 'Britain' are used interchangeably, which creates confusion. It also muffles English demands for a fair hearing of its interests. The result is a situation that comes dangerously close to violating the principle of 'no taxation without representation'. For example, under the famous 'West Lothian question' which Field explores, England co-finances Scottish spending, but without being able to weigh on political decision-making in these matters. In contrast, Scottish MPs are allowed to cast their votes in Westminster.

The unity of a 'demos' is threatened by a different form of divided loyalties, which have not been a principal focus in this book. Manifestations of religion can challenge not only representative government, but the state itself. The obvious example here is those young people in Western European countries, who pledge allegiance to radical Islam. It is important to ask whether Islam as a belief system is compatible with the nation state. Roger Scruton touches on the issue in his essay, and suggests that doubts remain, for a number of reasons. First of all, in societies where Islam is the dominant faith, unconditional loyalties take tribal and religious, but never a national form. Moreover, perhaps the nation state in itself is an anti-Islamic idea? Certainly that is what Sayyid Qutb, Egyptian intellectual and leading member of the Muslim Brotherhood would have had us believe. Living in 'the shade of the Qur'an', as he famously put it, you surrender to God, not to mortals. Indeed, this was the essence of the famous correspondence between the British High Commissioner in Egypt, McMahon, and Hussein bin Ali, the Sharif of Mecca in 1915. Sympathetic to the Arabs, McMahon advised them to quickly hammer stakes into territorial boundaries since he could see what was coming in the post-war carve-up. But Hussein explained that the Arabs simply did not see themselves or their identity in that way. The ummah, the commonwealth of the faithful, encompasses all Muslim believers, with the implicit and explicit task of conquering and converting ever more people. De facto, national boundaries and law made by men for men have no meaning. Against the Islamist backdrop of Qutb, who was executed in 1966 on charges of plotting to assassinate Egyptian president Nasser, it is not surprising that what political shape an Islamic state should or should not take is hotly debated, within and without the Islamic world.

Many Western commentators see radical Islam as a response of traditional Muslim societies to modernity. Olivier Roy, a French scholar of Islam, comes to a different conclusion. His subject is the monumental failure of making Islam as a religion adhere to the nation state in Western Europe. For him, present day Islamic fundamentalism is a product of Westernisation itself. This globalised Islam has long left behind its cultural and religious roots. Instead, it serves as an anchor for young second generation immigrants who feel as strangers in their host societies. Ironically, their demands for a pure and authentic Islam are nothing but a Western-inspired individual search for the meaning of life.

What could be an antidote to such estrangement, powerful enough to trump the voice of God? Many observers stress better integration into the economic life of a nation as a counterweight to fundamentalist lure. But, if Roy is correct, this only partly satisfies the yearning for individual acknowledgement and respect, which finds its expression in a globalised pop culture version of Islam.

Faced with challenges such as indigestible and

potentially threatening minorities, the nation state needs to be strengthened. Is there anything that could hold together the rents in the national fabric, which would be both extremely powerful, yet light as a spider's web? Edmund Burke once said that education was the cheap defence of a nation, and the authors of this book tend to agree.

In this volume, Christopher Husbands has explored history teaching and the role it plays in forging or re-forging a nation state. He is rightly dismissive of the idea of a 'usable past', as it would amount to nothing more than propaganda. He is nevertheless conscious that the learning of history shapes understanding of the present as much as of the past. Not surprisingly therefore, the formalised history curriculum has, since its inception in the nineteenth century been an ideological battleground. But without being directed, pupils may just pick and choose from the past to justify their preconceptions, which could reinforce conventional misunderstandings. Worse, such historical cherry picking risks widening existing gulfs between various societal groups, be they cultural or religious.

Nations need a national narrative, however clumsy that concept may sound. Ernest Renan, who saw us off on our sailing trip to explore the nation state, would violently agree. For him, nations are 'a daily plebiscite', as famously expressed during a speech at the Sorbonne in 1882. People must remember the great feats they achieved together in the past, in order to feel the urge to do great things together in the future. Perhaps surprisingly for a distinguished scholar of history, Renan also advocates partial forgetfulness. According to him, a selective memory is essential for a nation to feel as one. Certainly, at first glance, some events, and each country has episodes in its history not to be overly proud of, are best forgotten. But can they forever be swept under the carpet? Skeletons in the closet, big or small, have a nasty habit of making unwanted appearances, usually at the most unsuitable moment. Better to tackle controversial episodes of national history together, and in good time. In that fashion, whole stretches of the past, such as for example France's experience under German occupation and the compromised Vichy regime, which might otherwise linger, officially tarnished, in a corner can be salvaged through critical appreciation.

In a context of either unravelling or non-existent national loyalties, the best that can ever be achieved is what Jean Bethke Elshtain calls a '*modus vivendi*', an uneasy agreement to 'live and let live'. In this scenario, the state is reduced to nothing but a convenience store. It also is an awfully thin blanket to provide warmth and shelter to a political body, in real danger of being ripped apart by the first serious storm. Policy makers may still cling to conventional post-national wisdom, but people have never really given up on their privileged ties to both polity and community. There is a yearning to acknowledge the importance of patriotic affection in people's lives. While some might recoil from such 'identity politics', these demands will not just disappear; they are looking for political expression. The rise of Geert Wilders' Party, the Party for Freedom in the Netherlands, would be a case in point. Founded in 2005, advocating withdrawal from the EU and demanding assimilation of immigrants permanently living on Dutch soil, it is now the country's fourth-largest political party. Deemed at the far right of the political spectrum, it nevertheless is an expression of the very liberal nature of Dutch society. Its programme resonates with the Dutch people, which want to link acceptance of differences with respect for values deemed fundamentally important, such as equality of men and women, and tolerance itself.

It is ironic that England, the nation justly famous for inventing free speech and parliamentary democracy in the modern era, is treated as eccentric for wanting to take part in a political conversation regarding its very own future. Frank Field is of the opinion that lending a political voice to such legitimate demands is not only a sign of maturity but also of democratic strength. Up until now, Britain's ancient but largely unwritten constitution had adapted itself remarkably well to power moving from one institution to another, from the crown, to the House of Lords, to parliament and then to the cabinet, the 'elective dictatorship'. Devolution has put an end to that. An acknowledgement of that fact is a sheer necessity. The alternative, Field warns, is that extra- parliamentary forces are bound to take up those political debates denied to the voters; and that would be an alarming prospect.

So the point of being Leviathan is that at certain points, a will must be imposed on the many; and for this to be done safely, it must benefit from prior legitimation. So let us now have a look at the issue of state sovereignty.

Challenges to sovereignty

Given our interconnected and interdependent existence, what does sovereignty mean in today's world? Looking back through history, one quickly realises that it has never been possible to live in autarky and seclusion. Ever since human beings assembled in larger groups, their lives have been shaped by goods, people, services and information exchanged; wars fought and lost; treaties signed and broken; alliances assembled and fallen into disarray. In all of these cases, interdependencies – cultural, religious, political, economic, or military – have existed, and continue to exist.

Sovereignty, in its revolutionary shape hailing from the seventeenth century meant unchallenged authority domestically and unhampered pursuit of a country's interest in the international realm, including the right to wage war. In the wake of the Second World War sovereignty was curtailed, at least on paper. Since then, international law, in codified or non-codified form has encroached more and more on every state's rule over its citizens and residents. What concerns a country's prerogatives on the international scene, the Charter of the United Nations, a collective security organisation, proscribes war, and sees the use of violence as a last resort. But has that much really changed since 1648? States still are the main actors of the international system. They form the building blocks of international governance, whose institutions have to rely on the states to execute their writ. In the absence of a will to implement them, international norms are applied at best selectively. When it comes to sanctioning state behaviour for example, the five permanent members of the Security Council often behave according to the principle of 'one weight and (at least) two measures', preferring to protect client or allied states from international reprimand rather than upholding legal principle. So in the end, state power remains a decisive factor in who is called to heel and who gets a free pass.

As Daniel Hannan points out in this volume, it is mostly Western democracies that take international legislation seriously, while authoritarian governments are happy to give it short shrift. In Europe, ironically, this can have anti-democratic outcomes, for there appears to be a growing tendency of domestic courts to use international conventions to challenge decisions of elected governments. Problematically, international law exists outside of domestic accountability chains linking political with legal authority, framed by constitutional arrangement.[6] International courts are neither democratically constituted, nor democratically scrutinised. This means a reversion to the pre-modern notion that law-givers should be guided by their conscience rather than be accountable to those who must live by their decrees.

What has it meant for sovereignty, staunch pillar of democracy and freedom, to be a member of the European Union and to be subject to supranational law? The penetrating power of its legal instruments (regulations and directives), as well as of its jurisprudence rendered by the European Court of Justice is certainly something never experienced before. In his essay, Roger Scruton jokes that he has nothing against empire – provided it is organised like the Roman one, respectful of custom and tradition and providing an overarching framework establishing a civilisation. Not surprisingly, the author is of the opinion that the European Union achieves neither. Worse, by its very nature, supranational EU law questions perhaps the most fundamental achievement of Western Europe, secular jurisdiction, by definition bound by a specific territory. Therefore the attempt to build a European Empire of laws will not merely fail – it risks undermining the authority of secular law itself in the process.

Another area in which state sovereignty is challenged pertains to the realm of the economy. While it is not entirely clear what 'the market' is – Tom Kremer in his essay likens it to a football referee officiating at several different matches simultaneously that all have a bearing on each other – it is clear that market forces have circumscribed the nation state's room for manoeuver. This is well illustrated by the travails of the Eurozone, especially the desperate attempts to refinance the government debt of its more vulnerable members.

What we might perceive as a series of catastrophic events triggered by the fall of Lehman Brothers in 2008 is in fact the long shadow of an economic crisis that began with the Nixon shock in 1971, decoupling the dollar from gold, to be followed by the oil price shock in 1973. Then, for the first time, the post-war consensus model coupling economic growth with a generous welfare state failed to produce enough jobs. Rising unemployment tipped states into the red, states which in order to finance welfare benefits resorted to taking out more and more government debt or just printing money. While other sectors of the economy lagged, deregulation of financial markets in the 1980s provided a breathing space. It kicked off several boom decades for the financial services industry, lifting the paper boats of western economies in the process. Europe and North America had been able to ignore the fundamental unsustainability of such a government-debt financed system for a long time, as crises erupted mostly on the periphery. South America and Asia paid a hefty price in the 1980s and 1990s; but the chickens have now come home to roost. Called to tighten belts and submitted to austerity measures, the 'core' of the world economy is now tasting some of the bitter medicine it meted out to the periphery before.

Michael Ignatieff reminds us that citizens expect the state to shield them against the disruptive forces of the global market. Certainly, as he argues, patriotism is not a transaction and loyalty is not an insurance contract, but the patriotic attachment of citizens to the nation state is intimately linked to the state's protective functions. Legitimacy of democracy depends on this popular understanding of sovereignty. Voters of all political orientations have been clamouring for more state intervention in times of strong economic headwinds, while disavowing neither competition, nor the market economy. But given that capital can now be moved thousands of miles by a single mouse click thereby circumventing regulatory constraints in the process, is the nation state still capable of fulfilling this function? Interestingly, the consensus in this book has been not only that it can, but that it has to.

Financial markets are indeed global, ruthlessly assessing investment opportunities and forcing governments to provide attractive business conditions. But where should capital on the move turn to now? Both the periphery and the core are dealing with similar challenges – government debt and the financing of tasks delegated to the state, as well as the generation of employment and growth. All asset classes, from stocks, bonds, to more exotic financial derivatives linked to currencies or cereal prices, are currently more or less correlated, gold being the only exception. Basing investment purely on arbitrage, it appears, will be more and more difficult. What we are witnessing is the enormous destruction of wealth that, it turns out, had in reality existed only on paper. Martin Wolf, distinguished *Financial Times* columnist, just a trifle contrite, admitted as much when assessing the impact of financial markets deregulation on the 'real economy'.[7] Once the process that carries the ugly word of 'deleveraging' has come to an end (and that might take a while), the financial sector and other market participants will most likely have to go back to the bread and butter of investing – looking for sectors with real growth potential. And for that they need the certainty of jurisdictions where contracts can be made and honoured. Who produces this?

The market and the state depend on each other. It bears repeating that Adam Smith's 'invisible hand' orchestrating the free play of market forces relies on an institutional framework to organise economic activity. In the end, it is states that set the rules and it is states that uphold them. A true market economy without the existence of a state, and dare one say a democratic one, is unthinkable. The market needs the rule of law, something only a democratic entity can reliably uphold. This tiny detail is often overlooked, for example when investing in countries with authoritarian governments such as China, or Russia.

With the demise of communism, hordes of Western

advisers descended on Moscow, wholeheartedly convinced that liberalisation of the economy would magi-
cally create a level playing field among economic actors.
In similar starry-eyed fashion, it is occasionally assumed
that the Chinese 'socialist market economy' somehow
functions according to western market conceptions.
But such capitalism without the rule of law, especially
in an economy where riches, material or immaterial, are
there for the taking, naturally translates into the ruth-
less rule of robber barons under state protection. In order to do business in such 'transition economies' (and
one wonders where they are transitioning to), investors
have to arm themselves with the certainty that nothing
is ever certain and that money spent is no guarantee for
a return on investment. Just ask the owner of IKEA,
the Swede Ingvar Kamprad, battling against corrupt
practices in Russia. Or the American Bob Dudley, who
was ousted as TNK-BP President and Chief Executive, a joint venture linking a Russian firm, TNK and
British Petroleum. In 2008, he was forced to quit after
sustained harassment from Russian authorities and failure to get his visa renewed. And if he were still available to take questions, a conversation with the English
businessman Neil Heywood would be most interesting.
Heywood, who acted as an intermediary linking Western companies to powerful members of the Chinese no-
menklatura, paid for his connections to the wife of Bo
Xilai, the then Chongqing party chief, with his life.

Ironically, this oversight, that the market needs a

democratic state at its base to function properly, is also at the root of the ongoing Eurozone crisis, albeit in a different fashion. The Treaty of Maastricht of 1992, which introduced the single currency built a half-way house. As political integration leading to a true federal state was not on the cards in the early 1990s, senior politicians at the time opted for enhanced economic integration instead. The hope was that the completion of the single market and the launch of the euro would create the necessary impetus for further Europeanisation at the political level in the not too distant future. But by decoupling the economic from the political sphere, politicians created an inherently unstable situation, with systemic economic imbalances that have built up threatening to destroy the entire project from within. They also deprived themselves of political tools to intervene. The outcome is more than unpalatable: the euro has encroached upon the core functions of the nation state, weakening the sovereignty of the stronger and destroying the democracy and the economy of the weaker states. The political and the economic, separated at the birth of the euro, need to be reunited, either by creating a federal state, or by repatriating competencies to the national level.

Tom Kremer is convinced that the creators of the euro willingly accepted – indeed consciously willed – the possibility of a systemic crisis when they devised a currency without a state. In his essay, he invites us to accept the gravitational pull of economic and cultural forces. The common currency, far from bringing its members to economic and financial parity, has achieved the opposite: the gap between south and north is so vast that keeping them together in one currency is a pipe dream. The solution can only be a break up of the Eurozone, regrouping member countries into a northern and a southern Europe. 'More Europe', which has resulted from each crisis of the last sixty years, is for the first, and fatal time, not the most likely outcome.

In the world of twenty-first century realpolitik as seen by most of the authors, an important question not quite resolved is how sovereign states should relate to one another. If the legal output of international institutions is of questionable democratic legitimacy and international governance often fails at providing global public goods, what could be an alternative? What forms of loyalties are at stake when dealing with the outside world?

Michael Lind thinks that there is enough room for manoeuvre to solve collective action problems in an intergovernmental setting. A society of states, bound by common norms rather than a society of individuals is compatible with the views of most liberal internationalists. While one owes loyalty first and foremost to one's own nation state, this does not preclude an active, engagement with the rest of humanity. It just should not be at the expense of its own citizens. Lind would probably approve of the North Atlantic Treaty Organisation, a Western military alliance now counting 28 member states after enlargement to the East post-Cold War. Decisions can only be made unanimously, while each country retains complete sovereignty and responsibility for its own actions. For a treaty-based organisation acronymically derided as 'No Action, Talk Only' and variously pronounced either dead or dying, it has gotten quite a lot achieved – to date: in the famous words of its first Secretary-General, Lord Ismay, the Russians are still out, the Americans still mostly in, and the Germans more or less down. And all this without reneging on cherished principles such as democratic accountability and national sovereignty.

Garrett Wallace-Brown looks at international entanglements from a cosmopolitan perspective trying to reconcile the nation state with international law. For him, so-called 'neo-sovereigntists' commit a definitional and conceptual error couching sovereignty in terms of independence. Using the analogy of Homer's *Odyssey*, in which Odysseus willingly lets himself be tied to the mast of his ship to simultaneously hear and resist the enticing song of the sirens, he suggests that one can limit autonomy for the sake of self-determination itself. To function as a self-determined actor might require dependence and a reduction of independence. Between Lind and Wallace Brown there are important differences that warrant further probing. Lind is quite content to rely on countries to organise international engagements on a case-by-case basis. By contrast, Wallace-Brown imbues international organisations and the legal output they produce with the sort of civilising power able to tame states, propelling them toward the distant goal of a world society of individuals.

While we might still be busy pondering theoretical arguments regarding state sovereignty, Julian Lindley French is there to swiftly remind us of an uncomfortable reality – the twenty-first century seems set to be hyper-competitive and state-centric. The power of the US, the hegemon that had gathered Western Europe under its mantle thereby permitting its post-modern, conciliatory vision of the world to develop, is experiencing relative decline. Relative, as no other country will rival its assets taken together for the foreseeable future. The rising powers, in Asia or elsewhere, give short shrift to any attempts to constrain their might, neither internally, nor externally, through international regimes. They unapologetically pursue their national interest striving for domination, in much the same way as Western European states jockeyed to come out on top in the past.

Western European elite reactions to this new 'old' world are a confused muddle. Their preferred model for dealing with the uncertainties of a globalised world would be to give up sovereignty nationally: to empower supra- and international layers of governance on their behalf. It is hard to accept that such 'pooling' of sovereignty has not delivered the economies of scale and scope at international level that were hoped for.

How could the nation state be strengthened?

We live in trying times, fraught with uncertainties. But amidst economic and social turmoil and shifting geo-political forces, a consensus bridging political divides is emerging in Western Europe. While politicians and academics might be last to see it, the popular verdict is that the nation state is something to be treasured, not to be denigrated. For the peoples living under its pro-jection, this is good news. But to continue to enjoy the goods it can provide, the nation state's twin attributes, representative government and sovereignty, need to be reinvigorated.

The ongoing economic and financial crisis is forc-ing us to review critically the way in which politics have been orchestrated over recent decades. Day-to-day politics had increasingly become couched in terms of universal principles, thereby blurring the essentially confrontational nature of politics. Wherever there is a winner, some other party stands to lose. Officially guided by such worthy causes as equality and fairness, the fact that each political measure carries a price tag and that someone has to pay in the end could be con-veniently overlooked.

This is now no longer a possibility. Politicians will be forced to move away from abstract universal values to address concrete realities, namely what tasks should stay with the state to be financed collectively, and how each national economy can create enough resources to be able to do so. This return to reality may be bumpy, but it will bring back the zest to politics. Western nation states can take heart from the fact that at least they are disposing of a framework that cushions external shocks and provides the necessary social cohesion to implement painful reforms. The stronger the national consensus, the more resilient the social fabric should be. When dealing with divided loyalties within, no easy solutions exist. What clearly has not worked is the doctrine of official multiculturalism, one of the centrepieces of the post-national narrative. By denying the very existence of often very real cultural differences, such an approach amounts to cultural blindness. The result is a classic example of the road to hell being paved with good intentions. Multiculturalism neither encourages integration, for fear of upsetting cultural sensitivities, nor does much to foster social cohesion, as it leaves the host society without a clear understanding of what it actually stands for. Both parties remain petrified in their passive stance, one side not actively pursuing, the other side not actively demanding integration. Again, paradoxically, the current economic and financial heavy weather could deliver a cold shower of reality because in a crisis people take stock of what is truly important to them.

Winston Churchill reminds us saltily that 'If we open a quarrel between past and present, we shall find that we have lost the future.' Given the highly emotional and political nature such a debate on national history and national identity might assume, could a fight between past and present even be avoided? But this begs the question – would avoiding such a heated discussion stand a chance of bringing to life a workable future instead? If one has to pick one's battle and chose one's war, this fight looks like one worth fighting.

How could sovereignty be 'rebooted'? One key battleground certainly is the question of what takes priority: politics or economics? In his writings, Alain Touraine, a French sociologist, traces the relationship between the economy and the political over the course of the last two centuries. While the eighteenth century was characterised by a rupture between religion and the state, in the nineteenth century, politics and the economy bifurcated, only for the twentieth century to see the economy and society parting ways. What will happen in the twenty-first century? Will the state, society and the economy find a new, shared modus vivendi? One would certainly hope so. An economic system that, as some observers cannily put it, has privatised gains, while nationalising losses is clearly unsustainable, at least in democracies.

It would be naïve to assume that the nation state could go back to mercantilist and protectionist policies of eras long gone; but it is equally foolish to abdicate political responsibility, to deny the existing scope of action on the economic playing field. 'The market' certainly is a force to be reckoned with, especially when it comes to assessing a country's solvency and creditworthiness. But it would be premature to assume that the nation state has lost its ability to set the rules of the game, that the internationalisation of the financial system and the globalisation of value chains are inexorably forcing a race to the bottom in terms of regulation. Investment decisions are not merely driven by short-term speculative gains. Labour competitiveness in terms of skills, infrastructure, proximity to big markets, internal demand, social peace, the rule of law, are just a few factors determining financial flows. In this respect, the accumulated stock of a country's government debt constitutes a significant drag on its sovereignty. To become masters of their fate again, countries need to get their financial houses in order, a painful, yet necessary procedure.

What about sovereignty in the international realm? Here, it appears wise to strike a balance between engaging and protecting the very essence of the principle. Yes, certainly, international regimes are needed to look for solutions to problems that require collective action, to create and protect public goods. But such arrangements cannot be an end in themselves. Yes, norms contained in international law have an impact on state behaviour. But it would be unwise to disregard underlying power dynamics, as well as concerns regarding democratic accountability of international or supranational legislative activity.

If organisations that claim sovereign rights from member states stand revealed as pulling less than the weight of their component parts, if 'pooling' forces really amounts to shackling them, then such arrangements need to be critically reviewed. Governments in democracies govern on behalf of the people, and even if leadership and strategic vision might be unevenly distributed, at the very least, a debate on the subject is owed. Nothing that has been constructed at the hands of men cannot be undone by those very hands – even the supposedly sacrosanct 160,000 pages of *acquis communautaire*. In the end, the core of sovereignty, the final right of decision lying with the people has to be non-negotiable.

For the first time in 500 years, no European or European-inspired country can claim to dominate the world absolutely. The United States, the last super power standing, has to ration its direct interventions, and will be content to supervise regional balances of power in the future. Contenders for the role of global hegemon, benign or not, are waiting in the wings; power politics, a game Europe invented, and at which it excelled, is back. Time to dust off skills long forgotten, deemed obsolescent, or even dangerous. Time not only to master the many facets of foreign policy again, but to be better than the opponent. Hopefully all that knowledge still exists somewhere, in the dinosaur DNA of foreign offices, ministries of defense, intelligence agencies and chancelleries across Europe. One hopes it will be like riding a bicycle. More likely, European countries will have to learn statecraft and diplomacy again – the hard way.

Notes

1 Ludwig von Mises, *Omnipotent Government: The Rise of the Total State and Total War*, (1944).

2 'The pursuit of a remote and ideal object, which captivates the imagination by its splendour and the reason by its simplicity, evokes an energy which would not be inspired by a rational, possible end, limited by many antagonistic claims, and confined to what is reasonable, practicable, and just. One excess or exaggeration is the corrective of the other, and error promotes truth, where the masses are concerned, by counterbalancing a contrary error. The few have not strength to achieve great changes unaided; the many have not wisdom to be moved by truth unmixed. Where the disease is various, no particular definite remedy can meet the wants of all. Only the attraction of an abstract idea, or of an ideal state, can unite in a common action multitudes who seek a universal cure for many special evils, and a common restorative applicable to many different conditions. And hence false principles, which correspond with the bad as well as with the just aspirations of mankind, are a normal and necessary element in the social life of nations.' Lord Acton, 'Nationality', *The Home and Foreign Review*, 1862

3 Manent, P., *La Raison des Nations. Reflections sur la démocratie en Europe* (2006; Paris: Gallimard).

4 Bobbitt, P., *The Shield of Achilles: War, Peace, and the Course of History* (2003; London: Random House)

5 Seton-Watson, H., *Nations and States: an Enquiry into the Origins of Nations and the Politics of Nationalism* (1977; London: Methuen), p.xii.

6 Rabkin, J., *Law without Nations? Why Constitutional Government Requires Sovereign States*, (2005; Princeton: Princeton University Press).

7 Wolf, M., 'The conservative counter-revolution', *Financial Times*, 23 August 2010.

– Authors' Biographies –

Jean Bethke Elshtain, a political philosopher whose task has been to show the connections between our political and our ethical convictions, is the Laura Spelman Rockefeller Professor of Social and Political Ethics at the University of Chicago. Professor Elshtain was born in the irrigated farm country of northern Colorado and grew up in the small village of Timnath, Colorado (population 185). She attended public schools in Colorado. A graduate of Colorado State University (AB, 1963), Professor Elshtain went on to earn a Master's degree in history as a Woodrow Wilson Fellow before turning to the study of politics. She received her PhD from Brandeis University in Politics in 1973. She joined the faculty of the University of Massachusetts/Amherst, where she taught from 1973 to 1988. She joined the faculty of Vanderbilt University in 1988 as the first woman to hold an endowed professorship in the history of that institution. She was appointed to her current position at the University of Chicago in 1995. She has been a visiting professor at Oberlin College, Yale University, and Harvard University. She is the recipient of nine honorary degrees. Professor Elshtain was elected a Fellow of the American Academy of Arts and Sciences in 1996.

Dr Garrett Wallace-Brown is Senior Lecturer in Political Theory and Global Ethics in the Department of Politics at the University of Sheffield and is Director of the Centre for

Political Theory and Global Justice (CPGJ). He has consulted on projects for the World Bank, the Global Fund, the Russian Ministry of Health and the Swedish government, and has worked on various global health governance projects in Africa. His publications include works on cosmopolitanism, international law, globalisation theory, global justice, international political theory, transborder infectious diseases and global health governance. He has recently published *Grounding Cosmopolitanism: From Kant to the Idea of a Cosmopolitan Constitution* (Edinburgh University Press, 2009), co-edited *The Cosmopolitanism Reader* (Polity, 2010) with David Held, and is currently in the process of publishing *Global Health Policy* (Wiley-Blackwell, 2012).

Frank Field has been a Member of Parliament for Birkenhead since 1979. His latest piece of work was a report to the Prime Minister on *The Foundation Years: Preventing Poor Children Becoming Poor Adults*.

Daniel Hannan is a writer and journalist, and has been Conservative MEP for South East England since 1999. He speaks French and Spanish and loves Europe, but believes that the European Union is making its constituent nations poorer, less democratic and less free.

Professor Chris Husbands is director of the Institute of Education, University of London. He read history and completed a doctorate at the University of Cambridge before beginning his career teaching in secondary schools. He was a teacher and senior manager in urban comprehensive schools before moving into higher education; he was formerly Director of the Institute of Education at Warwick University and Dean of Education and Lifelong Learning at the University of East Anglia. He is currently a Board Member at the Training and Development Agency for Schools, and a member of the advisory Learning Panel at the National Trust; he has also served as a Board member at two examining groups, Edexcel and the Assessment and Qualifications Alliance. He has worked as a consultant or adviser to local authorities, OFSTED, the DfE, the Qualifications and Curriculum Authority and the National College for Leadership in Schools and Children's Services; internationally he has worked with the Ministry of Higher Education in Dubai, the Ministry of Education in Egypt and with Microsoft Education in Taiwan.

Professor Husbands has research interests in teacher education and education policy. He was director of the National Evaluation of Children's Trusts, which explored the relationships between teachers and other professionals in supporting children's well-being (2004–8), led a review of children's outcomes in high-performing education systems for the Department for Education (2008–9) and the evaluation of the national development programme for directors of children's services. He led the UK component of the International Alliance of Leading Education Institutes' report on *Transforming Teacher Education* (2008) and on education and climate change (2009). He has written widely on aspects of education policy and on curriculum and teacher development and retains an interest in the teaching and learning of history.

Michael Ignatieff is a writer, teacher and former politician. Born in Canada, educated at the University of Toronto and Harvard University, he has written seventeen books and has worked as a television presenter and documentary film maker, editorial columnist and university teacher. He has taught at the University of British Columbia, Cambridge University, the London School of Economics and Harvard University, where he was Director of the Carr Center for Human Rights Policy at the Kennedy School of Government between 2000 and 2005.

He is the author of *The Needs of Strangers* (1984), *Scar Tissue* (1992), *Isaiah Berlin* (1998), *The Rights Revolution* (2000), *Human Rights as Politics and Idolatry* (2001), *The Lesser Evil: Political Ethics in an Age of Terror* (2004) and *True Patriot Love* (2009).

Between 2006 and 2011, he was Member of Parliament for Etobicoke Lakeshore, Deputy Leader and Leader of the Liberal Party of Canada. For the academic year 2011–12, he was Senior Resident at Massey College, University of Toronto. He is a member of the Queen's Privy Council for Canada and holds eleven honorary degrees.

Thomas Kremer was born in Transylvania. He survived the concentration camp of Bergen-Belsen and fought in Israel's war of independence. After reading Philosophy at Edinburgh University, he carried on post-graduate research at the Sorbonne and King's College in London.

Having pioneered game-based therapy for disturbed children, he designed a range of educational games adopted by primary schools throughout the UK. As a professional inventor, Thomas Kremer has created over 250 games and toys now widely distributed in all international markets.

He is the chairman of numerous middle-sized companies he himself founded over the years in Britain, Germany, France and the US. Chief among them is an ideas laboratory that is now the leader in its field in Europe.

Author of the critically acclaimed *The Missing Heart of Europe*, he has now turned his attention to publishing with a focus on trying to resurrect the art of the essay. Thomas Kremer and Lady Alison, his wife, live in a minor Elizabethan manor house in Devon, restored to something like its original glory through 25 years of deeply satisfying labour.

Michael Lind is Policy Director of New America's Economic Growth Program. He is a co-founder of the New America Foundation, along with Ted Halstead and Sherle Schwenninger, and was the first New America fellow. With Ted Halstead he is co-author of *The Radical Center: The Future of American Politics* (Doubleday, 2001) and the author of the first New America Press book, *Made in Texas: George W. Bush and the Southern Takeover of American Politics* (New America/Basic Books, 2003). Among his other nonfiction books are *The American Way of Strategy* (Oxford University Press, 2006) and *What Lincoln Believed* (Doubleday, 2005). Mr Lind has taught at Harvard University and Johns Hopkins and writes frequently for the *Financial Times*, *The New York Times*, *Democracy Journal* and other publications. He has appeared on C-SPAN, National Public Radio, CNN, the Business News Network, the Newshour and other programs. He has a weekly column in *Salon Magazine*.

Mr Lind's first three books of political journalism and history, *The Next American Nation: The New Nationalism and the Fourth American Revolution* (Free Press, 1995), *Up From Conservatism: Why the Right Is Wrong for America* (Free Press, 1996) and *Vietnam: The Necessary War* (Free Press, 1999), were all selected as *New York Times* Notable Books. He has also published several volumes of fiction and poetry, including *The Alamo* (Houghton Mifflin, 1997), which the *Los Angeles Times* named as one of the Best Books of the year, and a prize-winning children's book, *Bluebonnet Girl* (Henry Holt, 2004).

Julian Lindley-French, PhD, MA (Dist.), MA (Oxon.), is Eisenhower Professor of Defence Strategy at the Netherlands Defence Academy, a member of the Strategic Advisory Group of the Atlantic Council of the United States, Fellow of Respublica in London, Associate Fellow of Chatham House and of the Austrian Institute for European and Security Studies, as well as a Senior Associate Fellow of the Defence Academy of the United Kingdom.

Professor Lindley-French is a member of the Strategic Advisory Panel of General Sir David Richards, Chief of the Defence Staff in London and Head of the Commander's Initiative Group (CIG) for NATO's Allied Rapid Reaction Corps (ARRC). A Strategic Programme Advisor for Wilton Park, he is also a member of the Academic Advisory Board of the NATO Defence College in Rome.

He was formerly Special Professor for Strategic Studies at Leiden University and a Course Director at the Geneva Centre for Security Policy. He was European Co-Chair of the US-European Working Group on Stabilisation and Reconstruction Missions for CSIS and Project Leader for the Atlantic Council's Stratcon 2010 project on the NATO Strategic Concept.

Born in Sheffield, Yorkshire, England, in 1958, he is an Oxford historian and Oxford Blue. He received a Masters Degree in International Relations (with distinction) from UEA and holds a doctorate in political science from the European

University Institute. He has lectured in European Security at the Department of War Studies, Kings College London, and therein was Deputy Director of the International Centre for Security Analysis (ICSA). He was Senior Research Fellow at the EU Institute for Security Studies in Paris and acted as a senior advisor to the NATO Secretary-General in Brussels, where in 1999 he was recognised for outstanding service.

In January 2007 he published a new book entitled *NATO: The Enduring Alliance* with Routledge in the US and Europe. In January 2008 he published a book on the history of European defence with Oxford University Press, which was nominated for the Duke of Westminster Medal for Military Literature. In April 2010 he published *A New Alliance for a New Century* in Washington for the Atlantic Council. In November 2010 he published a new Whitehall Report for RUSI entitled *Between the Polder and a Hard Place – The Netherlands Armed Forces and Defence Planning Challenges for Smaller European Countries*. In December 2010 he published a major paper for Chatham House entitled *Britain and France: A Dialogue of Decline?* and in October 2011 published another report for Chatham House on *Strategic Communications and National Strategy* with Professor Paul Cornish of Bath University. In February 2012 he published the *Oxford Handbook on War* (Oxford University Press) with Professor Yves Boyer of the Ecole Polytechnique in Paris, which has also been nominated for the Duke of Westminster Medal. He is currently preparing a book on British national strategy with William Hopkinson, a former senior official at the Ministry of Defence.

Johanna Möhring is Visiting fellow at the Mackinder Programme for the Study of Long-Wave Events, London School of Economics and Political Science. She has previously worked in the Office of the Secretary General at the North Atlantic Treaty Organisation (NATO), as a private-sector consultant advising foreign investors entering the Russian market and at the Organisation of Economic Co-operation and Development (OECD), focusing on questions of governance and economic development. Ms Möhring, a German national, graduated from the University of Constance, Germany, with a master's degree in Public Administration/Public Policy. She holds an MA from the Johns Hopkins University, Washington, DC, in International Relations, as well as a degree in Slavic Studies from the 'Institut National des Langues Orientales' (INALCO), Paris, France.

Professor Gwythian Prins is a research professor at the London School of Economics and the director of the LSE Mackinder Programme for the Study of Long Wave Events. He joined LSE in 2000 successively as Professorial Research Fellow and then (2002–7) took the first stint as the first Alliance Research Professor jointly at LSE and Columbia University, New York. For over twenty years previously he was a Fellow, Tutor and the Director of Studies in History at Emmanuel College, Cambridge. He was a University Lecturer in Politics. He directed the Cambridge University military education programmes in the 1980s. During the later 1990s he served as Senior Fellow in the Office of the Special Adviser on Central and Eastern European Affairs, Office of the Secretary-General of NATO, Brussels. Simultaneously he was Senior Research Fellow at the Royal Institute of International Affairs, Chatham House, and served as the Visiting Senior Fellow in the (former) Defence Evaluation and Research Agency of the UK Ministry of Defence, Farnborough. He first published on climate security issues in 1986 and was the Consultant on Security at the Hadley Centre for Climate Prediction and Research of the British Meteorological Office for four years to 2003. His writing includes books in African history and anthropology, on strategy and geo-politics, and collaborative work on climate issues and a book (*Another Europe*, 2008) on the irreconcilable tensions between two visions of Europe, co-authored with Johanna Möhring.

Roger Scruton is an adjunct scholar of the American Enterprise Institute in Washington, DC, a new position he took up in July 2009. Prior to that he was a research professor for the Institute for the Psychological Sciences. He is also a fellow of Blackfriars Hall in Oxford.

He is a writer, philosopher and public commentator who has specialised in aesthetics with particular attention to music and architecture. He engages in contemporary political and cultural debates as a powerful conservative thinker and polemicist. He has written widely in the press on political and cultural issues. Three books were published in 2009: *Beauty* (Oxford University Press), *Understanding Music* (Continuum) and *I Drink Therefore I Am* (Continuum).

Other recent books are *England: an Elegy* (Continuum, 2006), an attempt to give identity to the idea of England and a tribute to its values and institutions; *Death-Devoted Heart: Sex and the Sacred in Wagner's Tristan and Isolde* (Oxford University Press, 2003), an analysis of the musical and spiritual meaning of Wagner's work; *News from Somewhere: On Settling* (Continuum, 2005), an evocative account of the author's attempt to put down roots in rural Wiltshire; *A Political*

Philosophy (Continuum, 2006), a thoughtful response to the development and decline of Western civilisation; *The West and the Rest* (ISI Books, 2003), an analysis of the values held by the 'West' and how they are distinct from those held by other cultures; *Gentle Regrets* (Continuum, 2006) and *On Hunting* (Random House, 1998), two autobiographical works; *Culture Counts: Faith and Healing in a World Besieged* (Encounter Books, 2007), an exploration of culture and why it matters; and a third edition of *A Dictionary of Political Thought* (Palgrave Macmillan, 2007), a concise and comprehensive collection of definitions for political thought and processes.